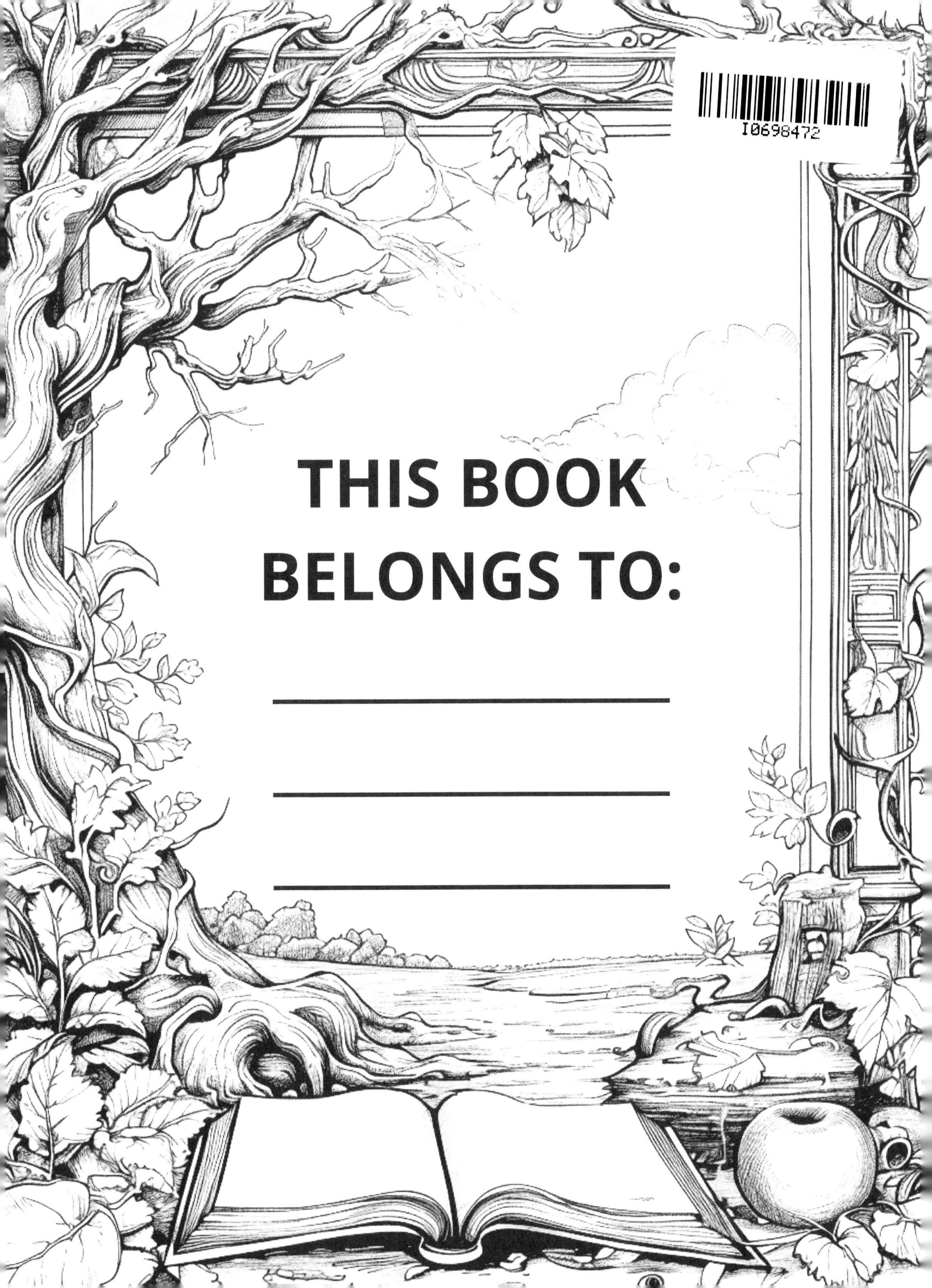

THIS BOOK BELONGS TO:

____

____

____

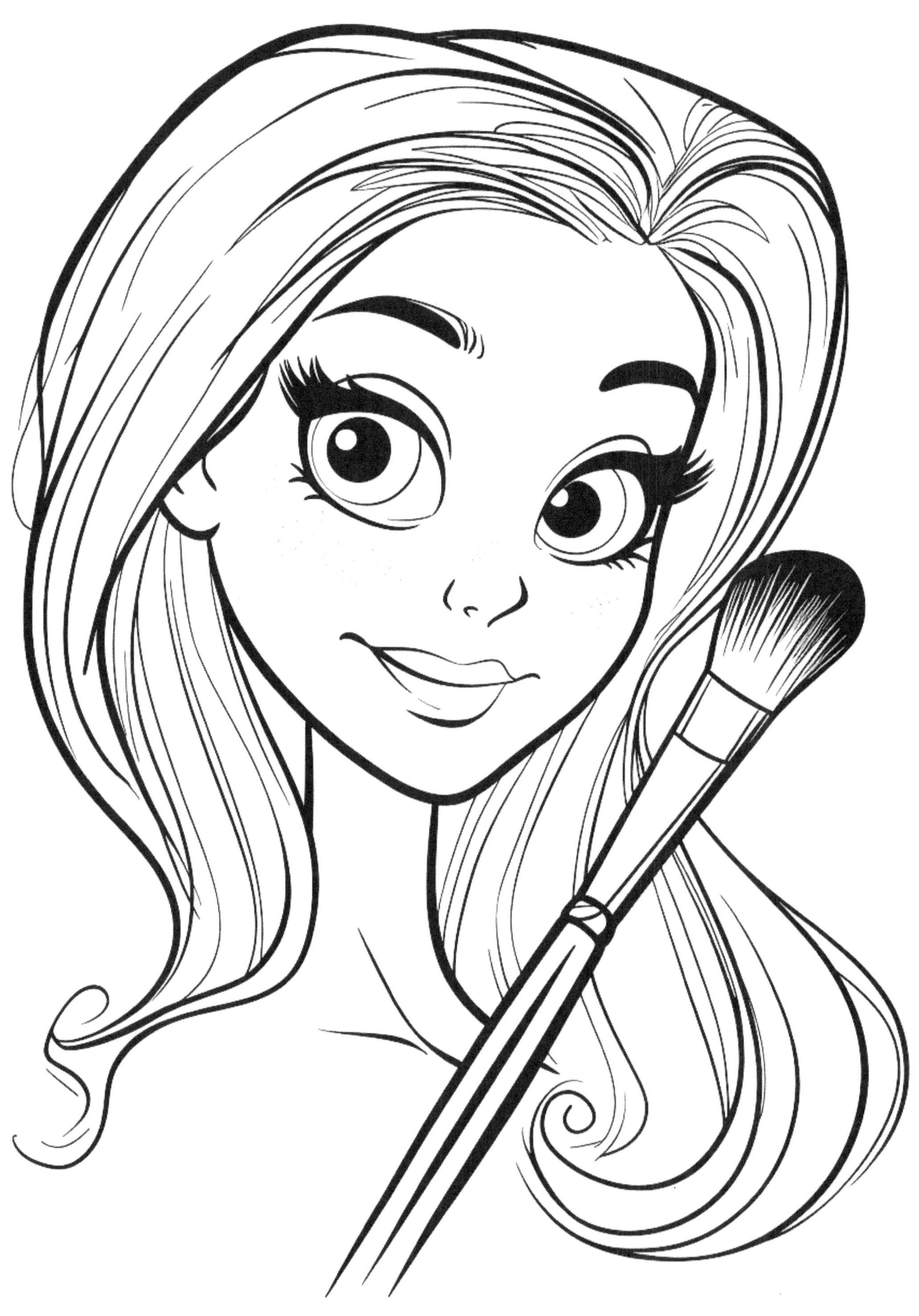

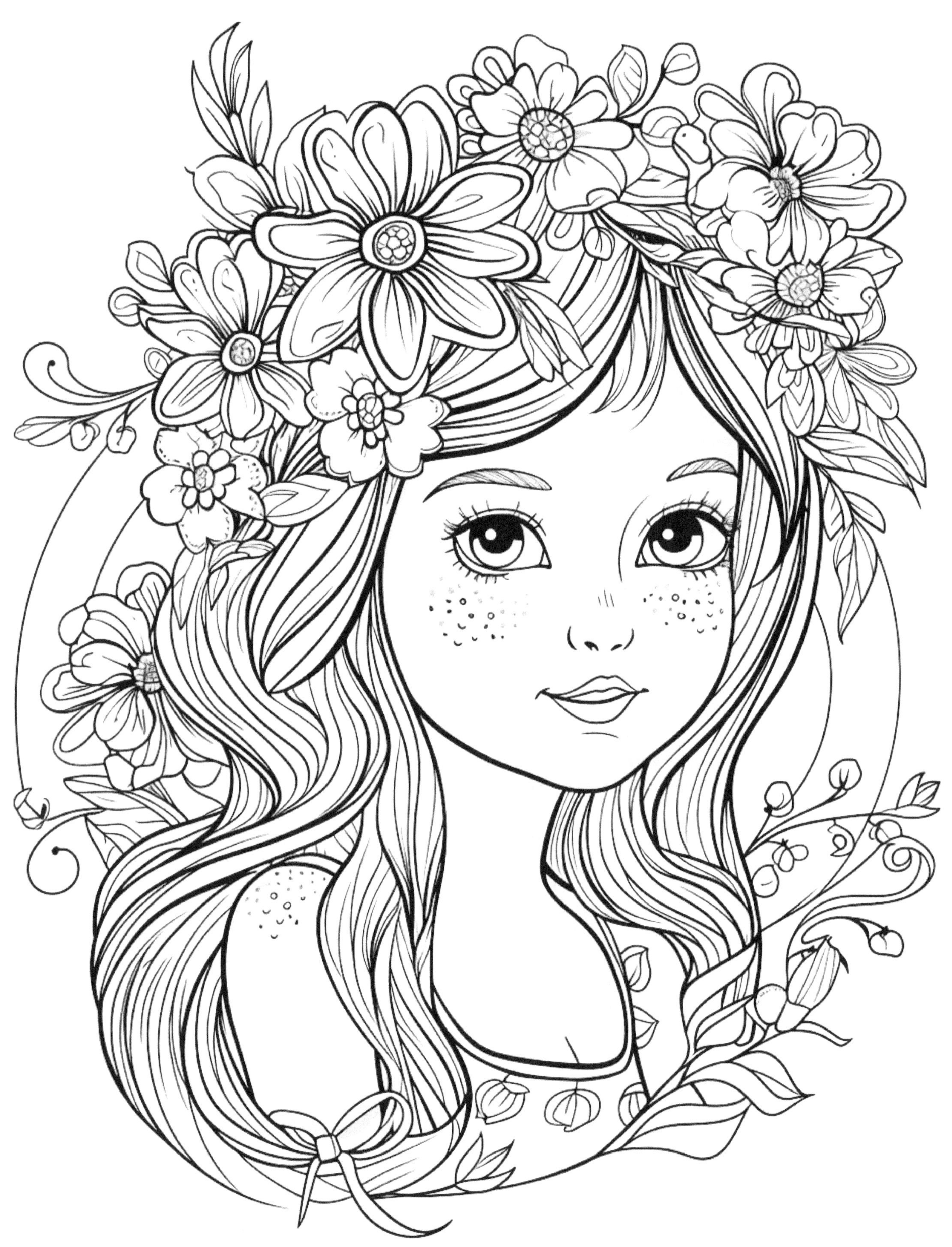

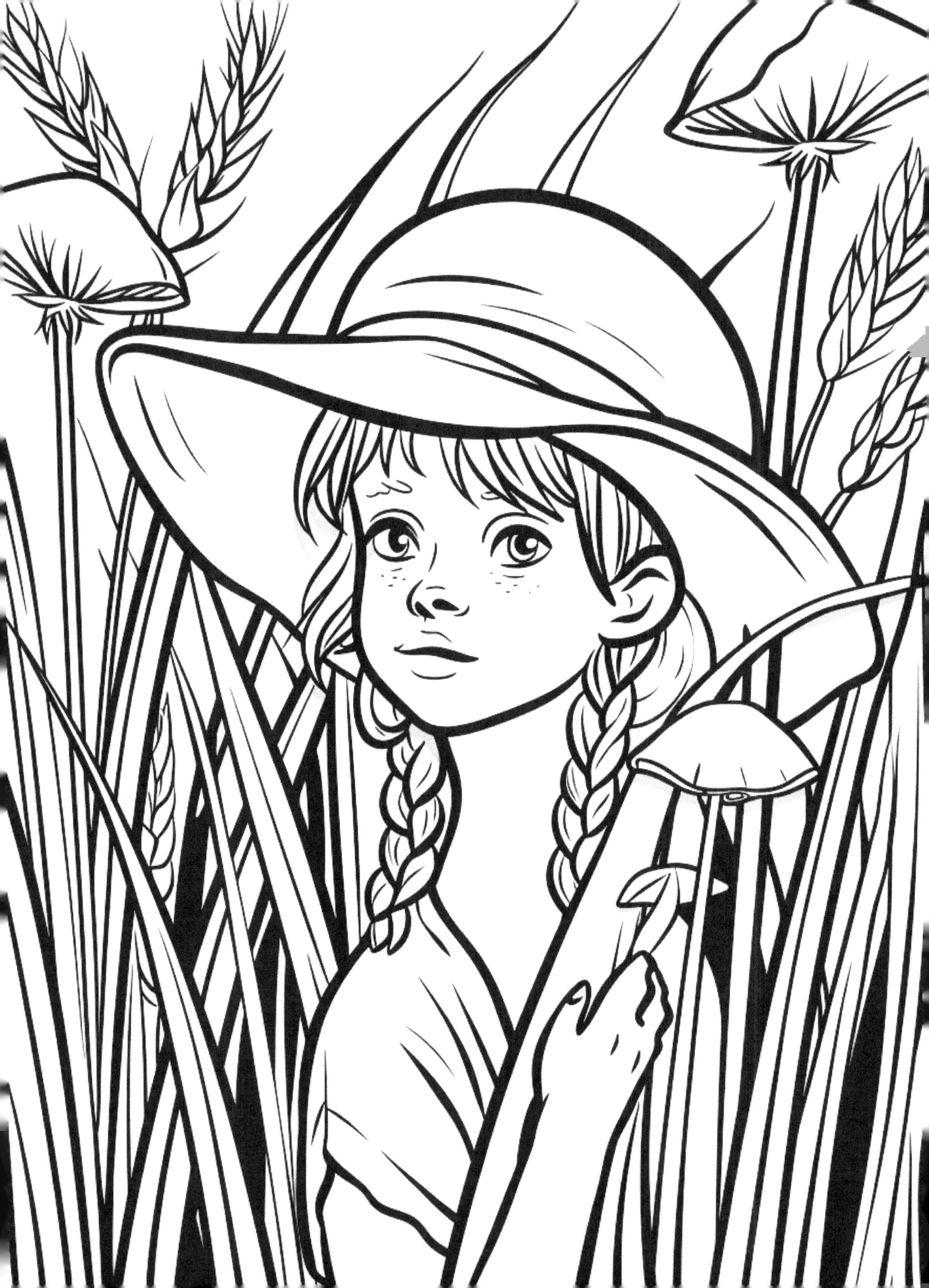

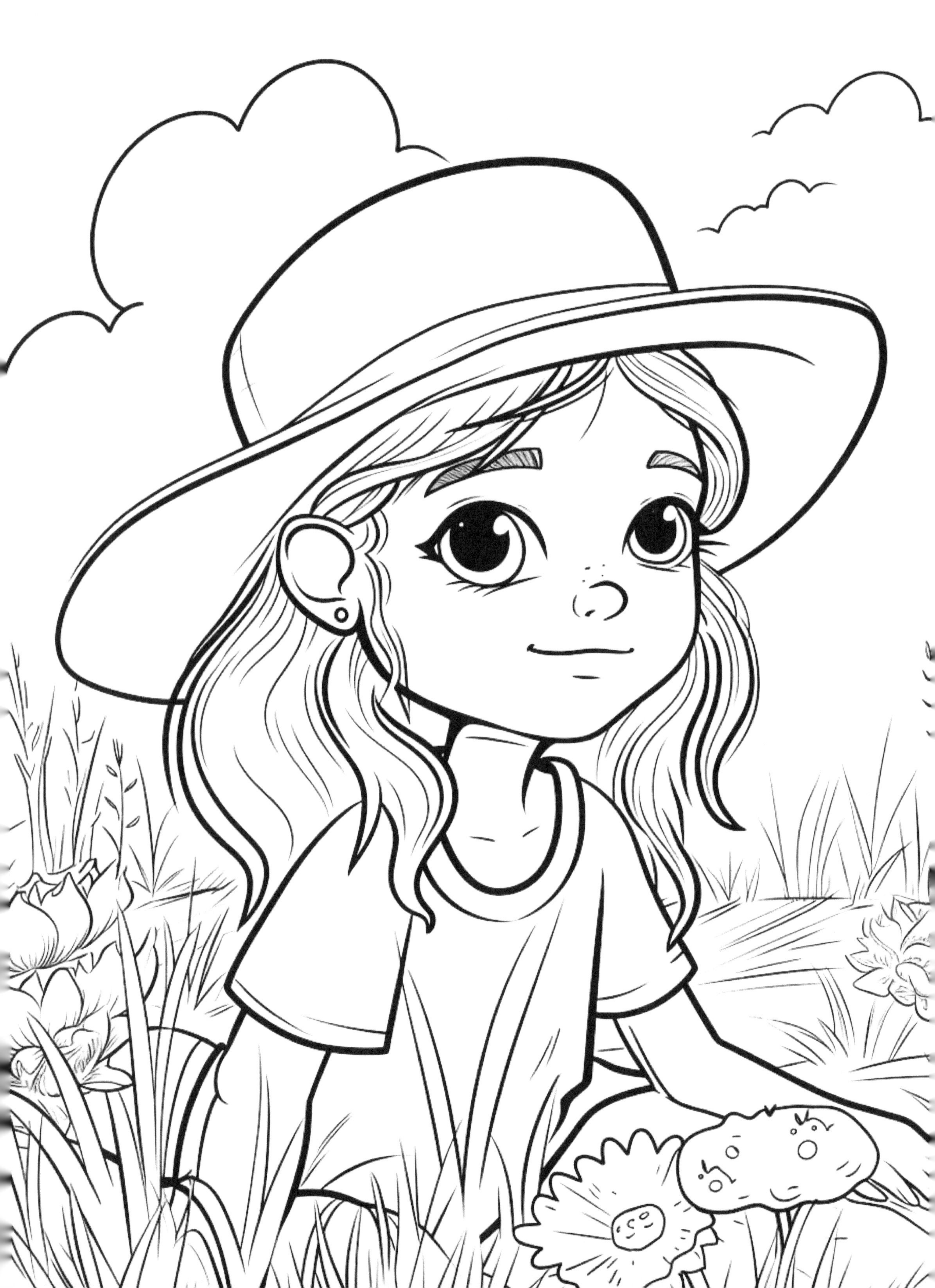

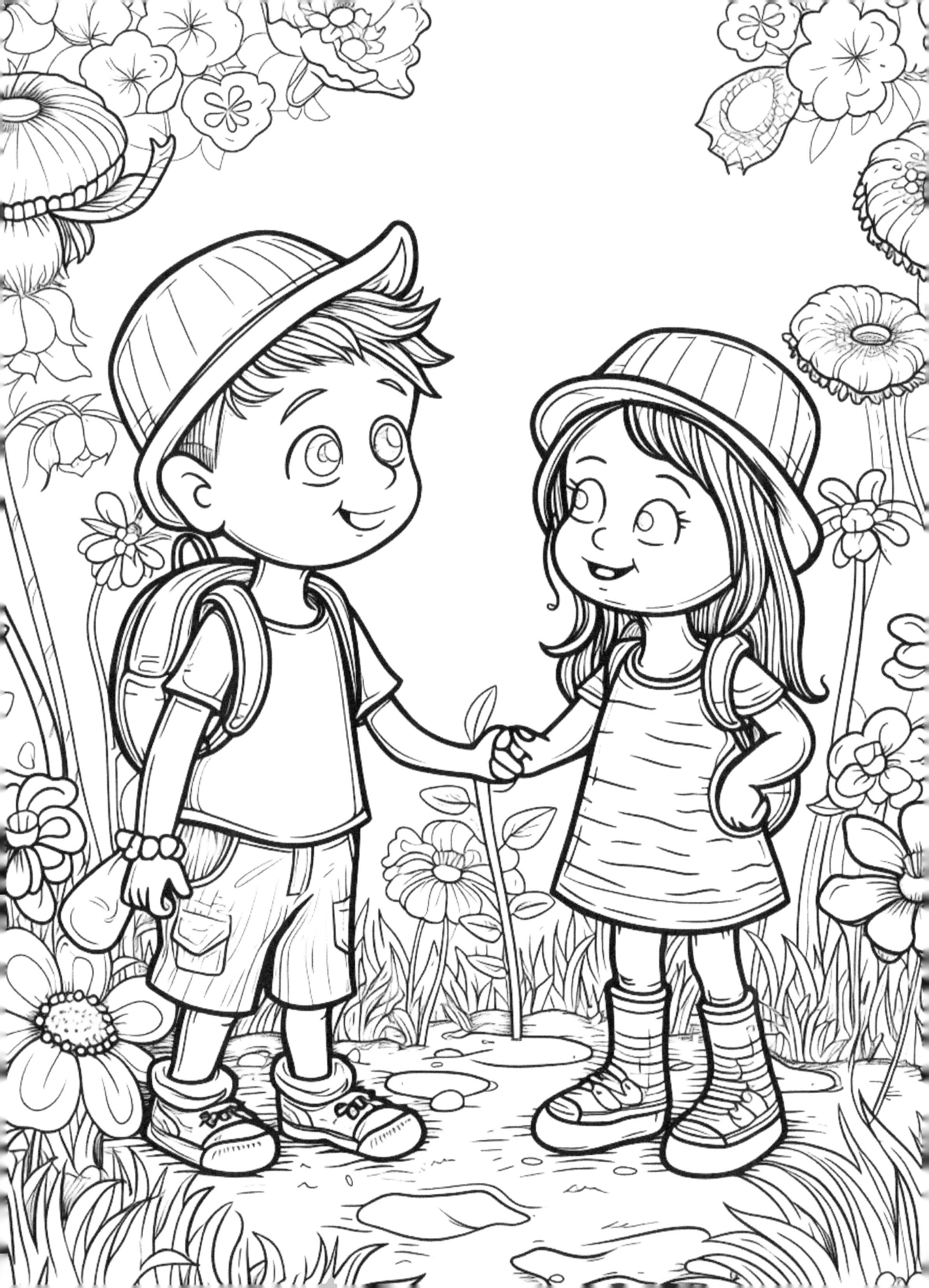

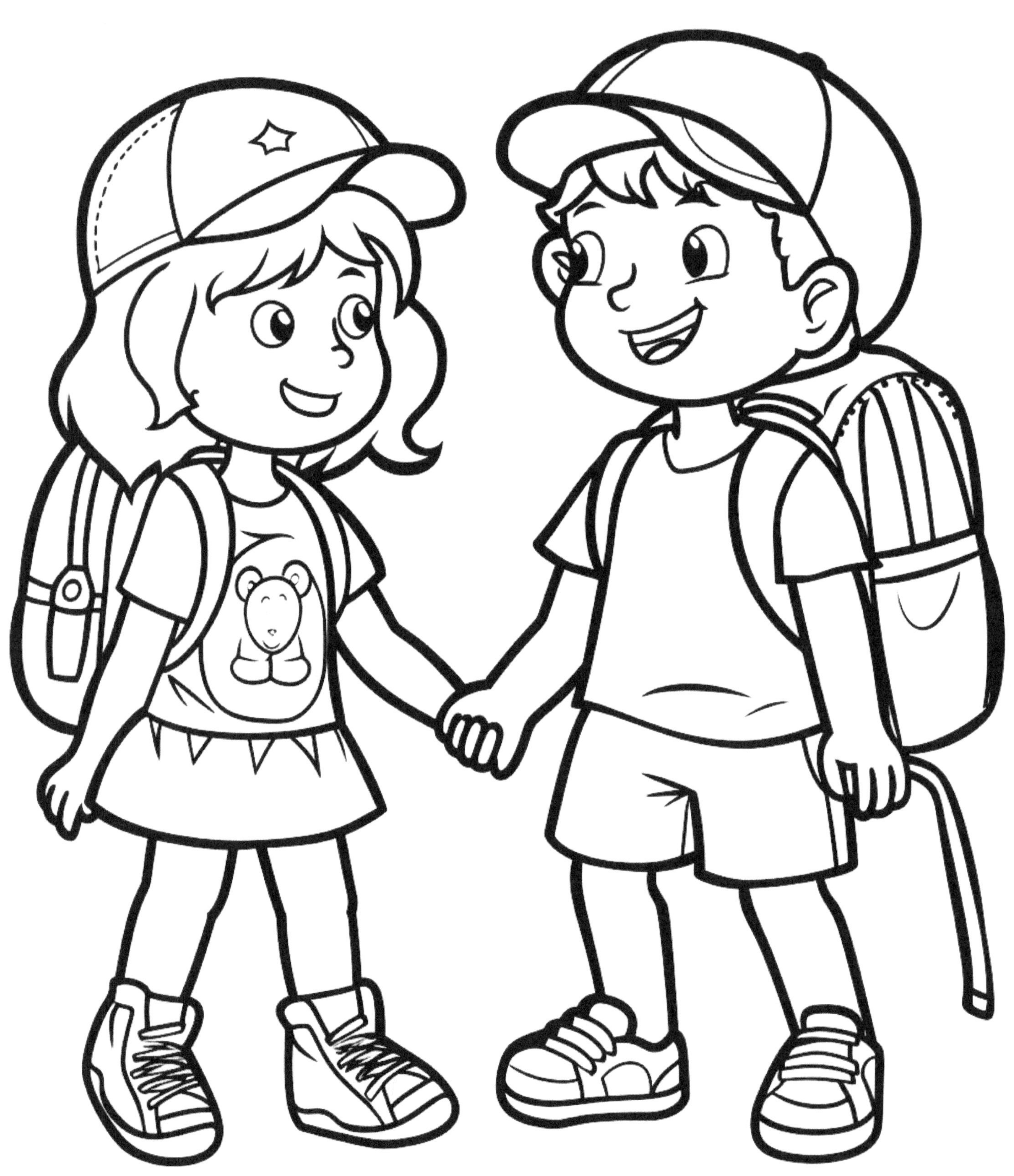

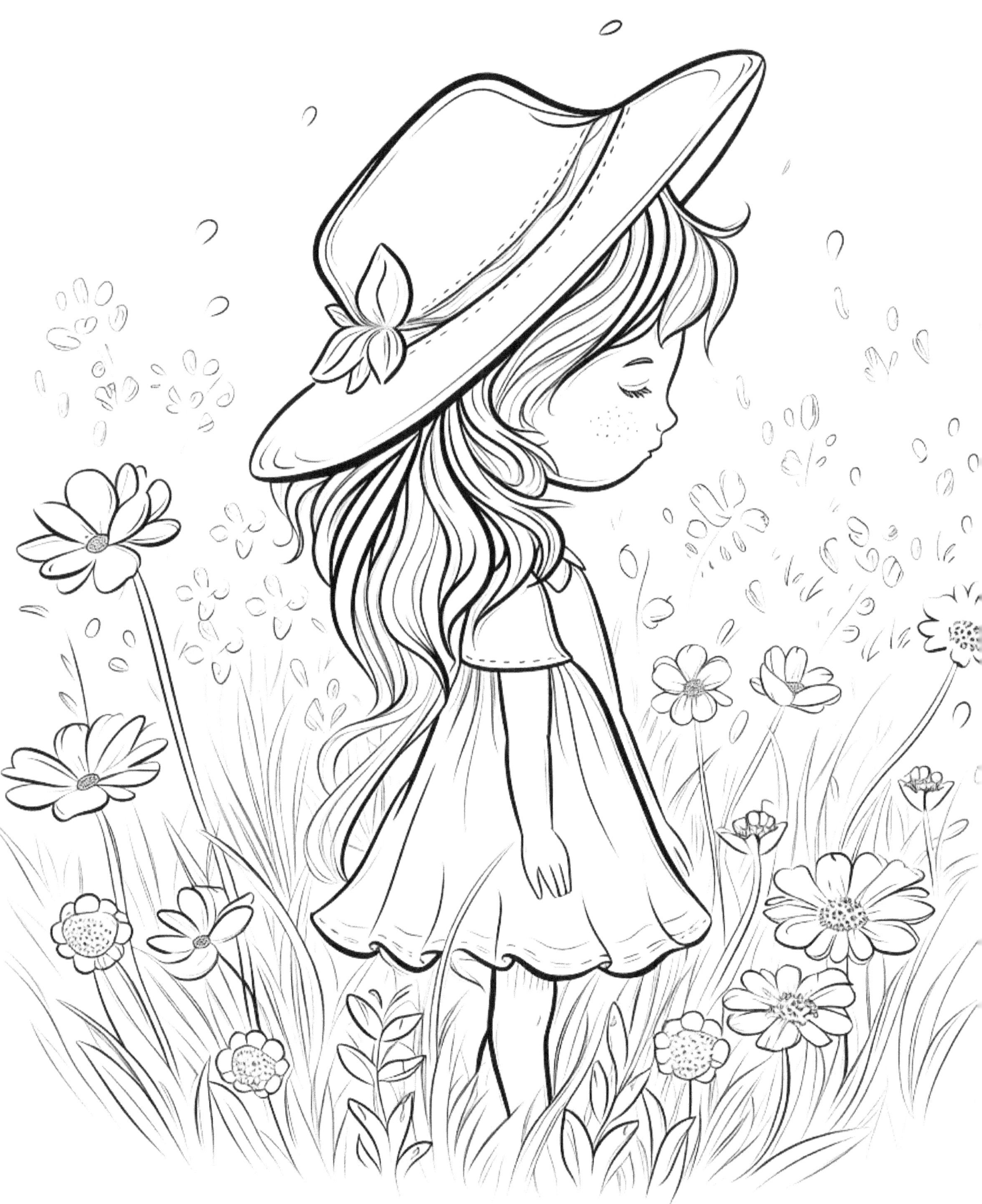

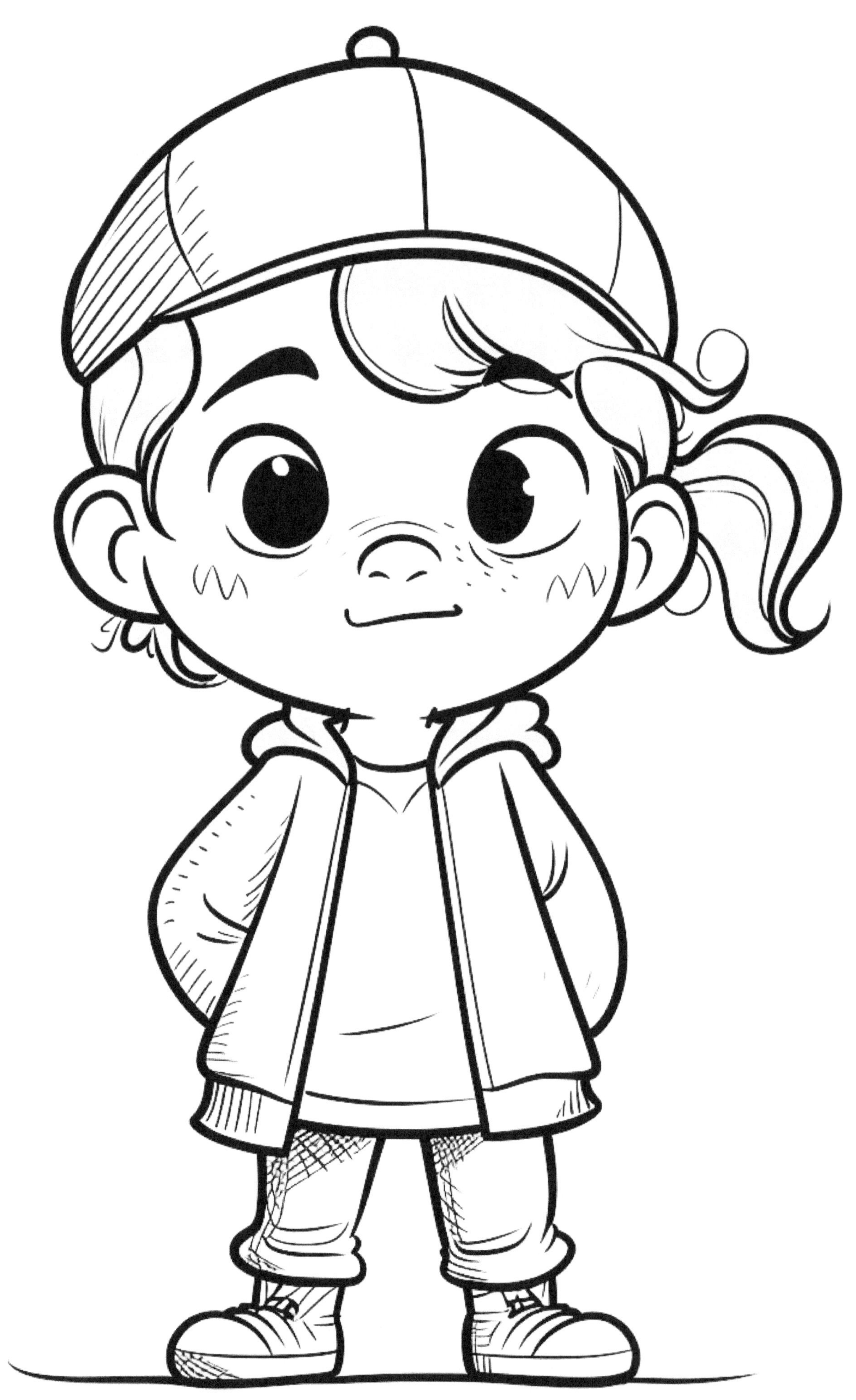

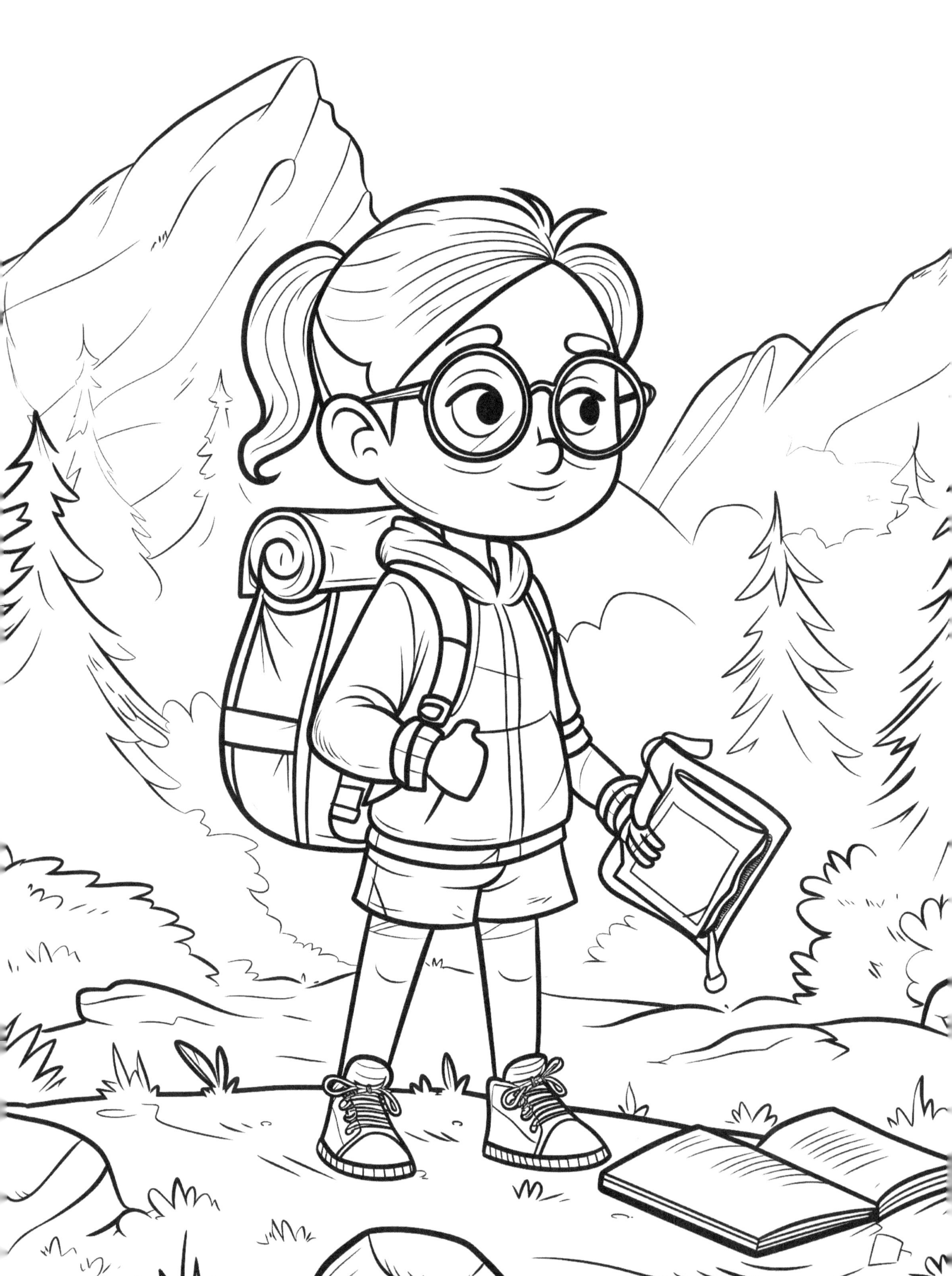

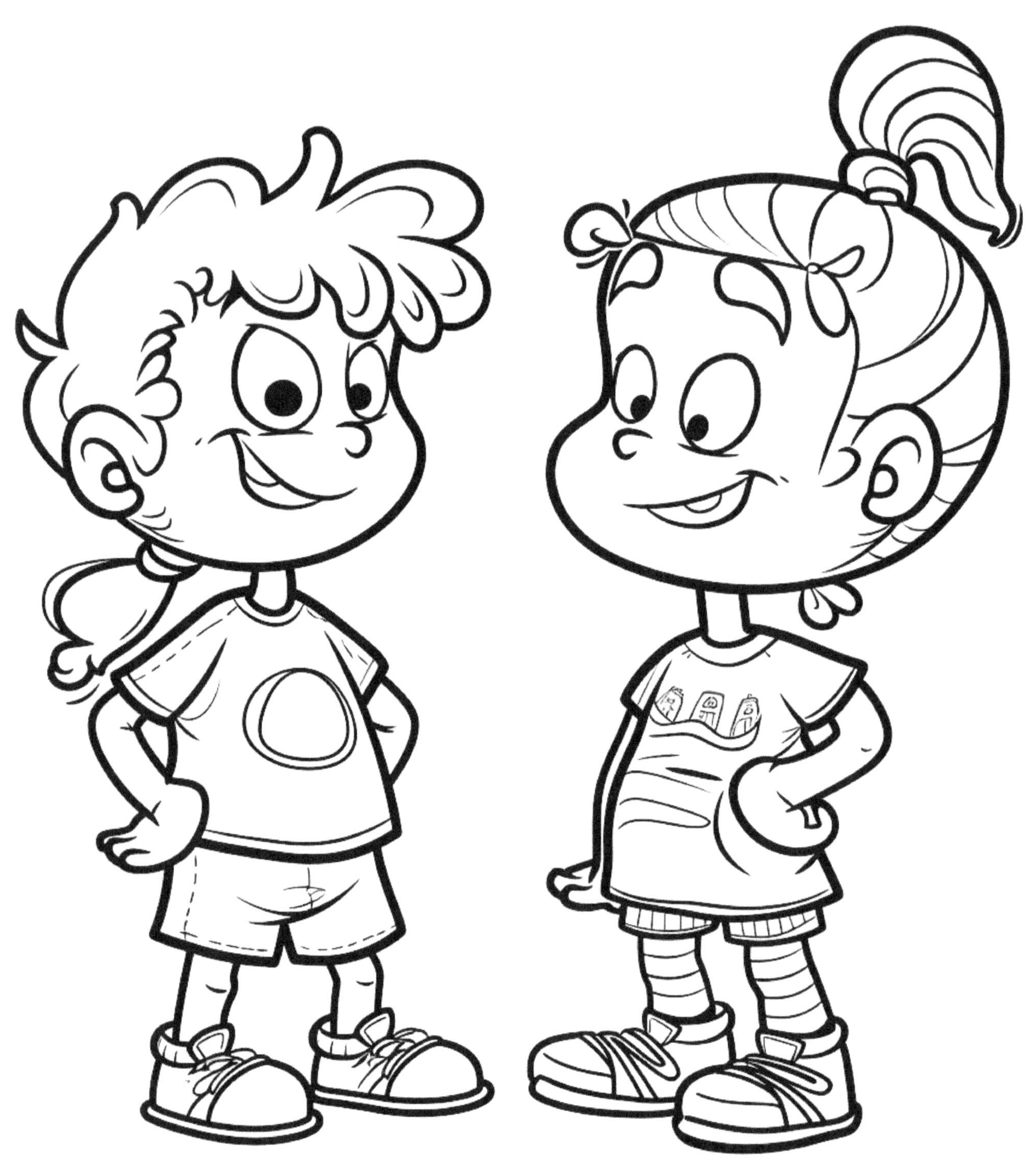

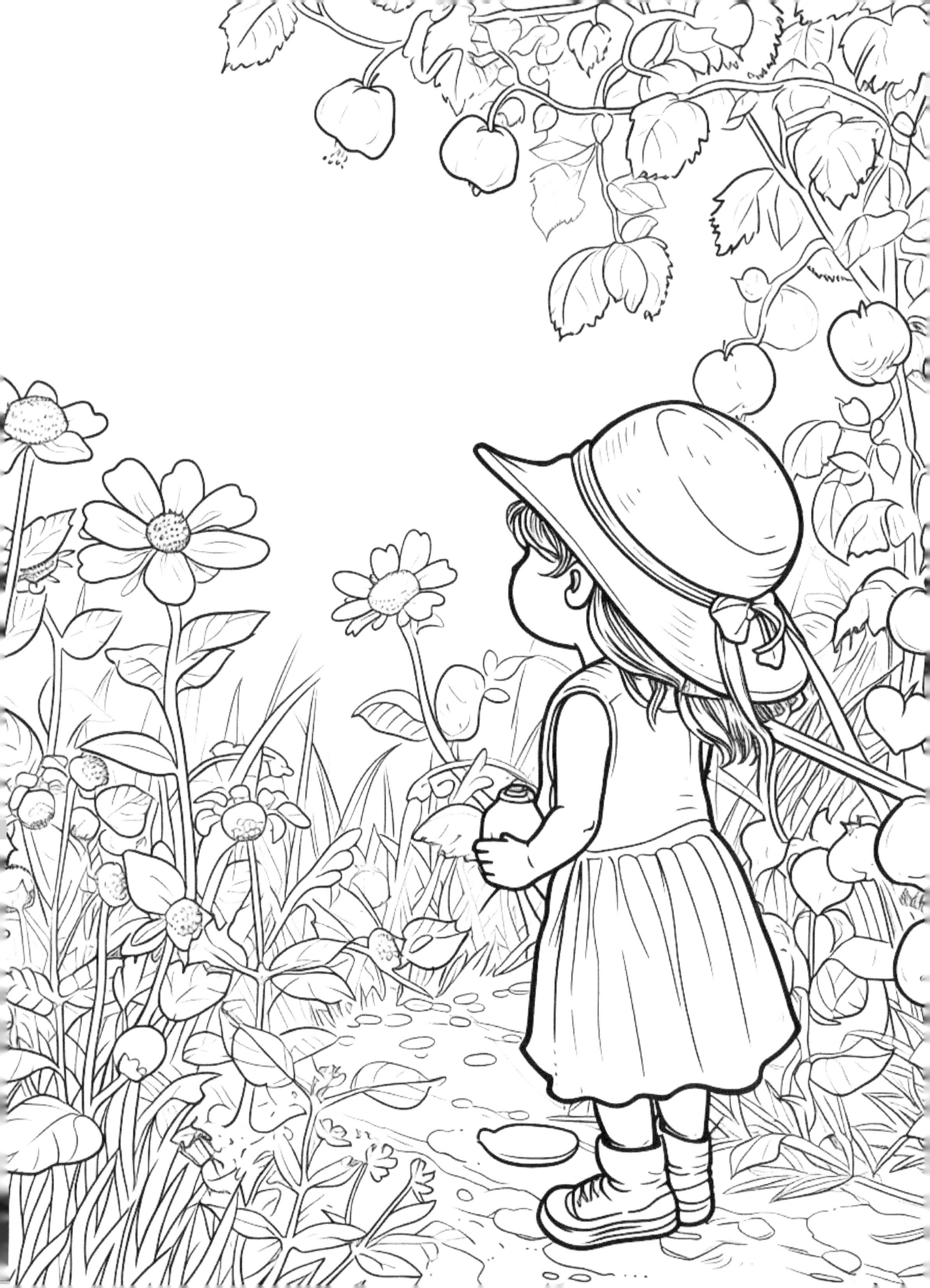

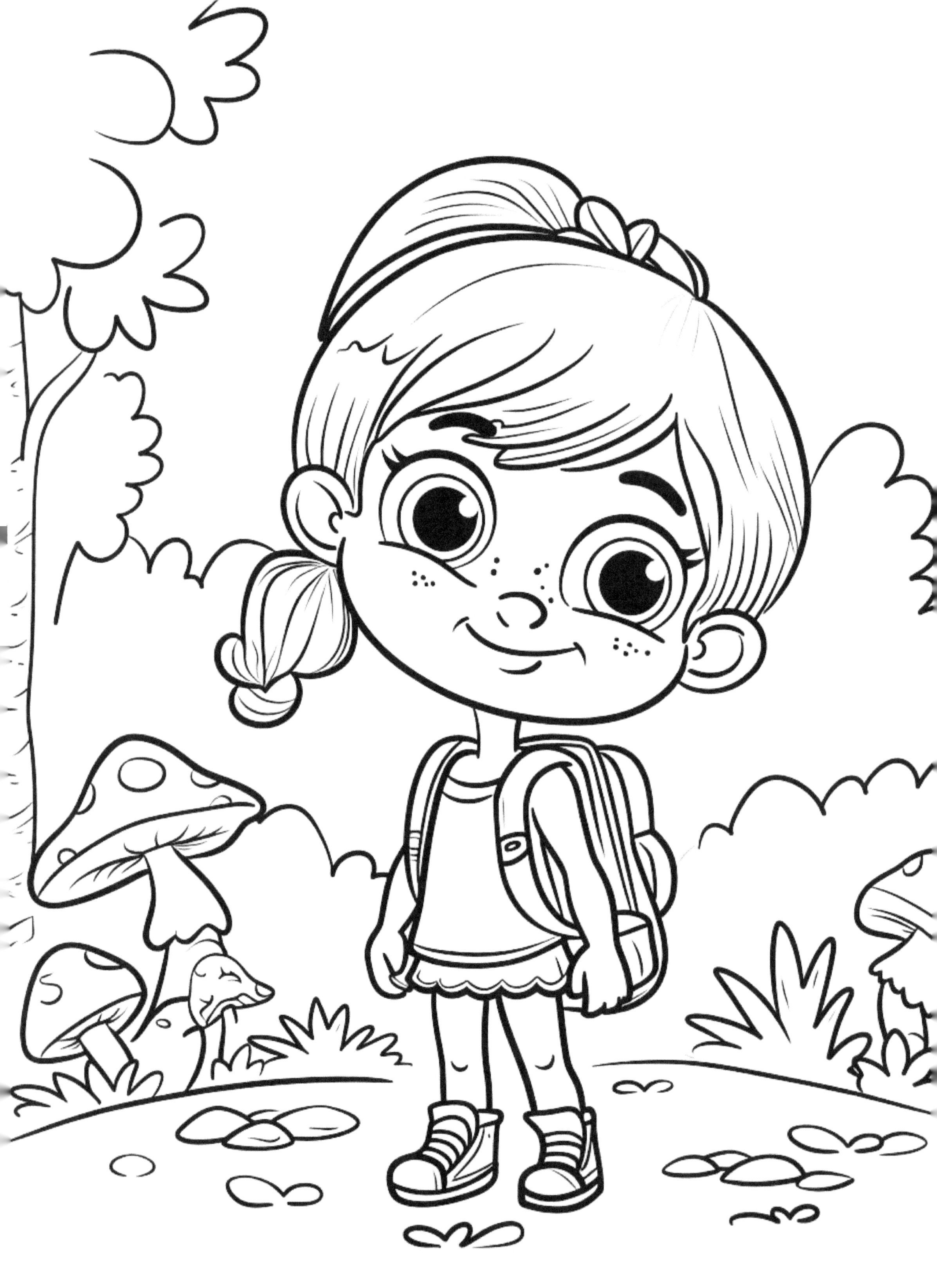

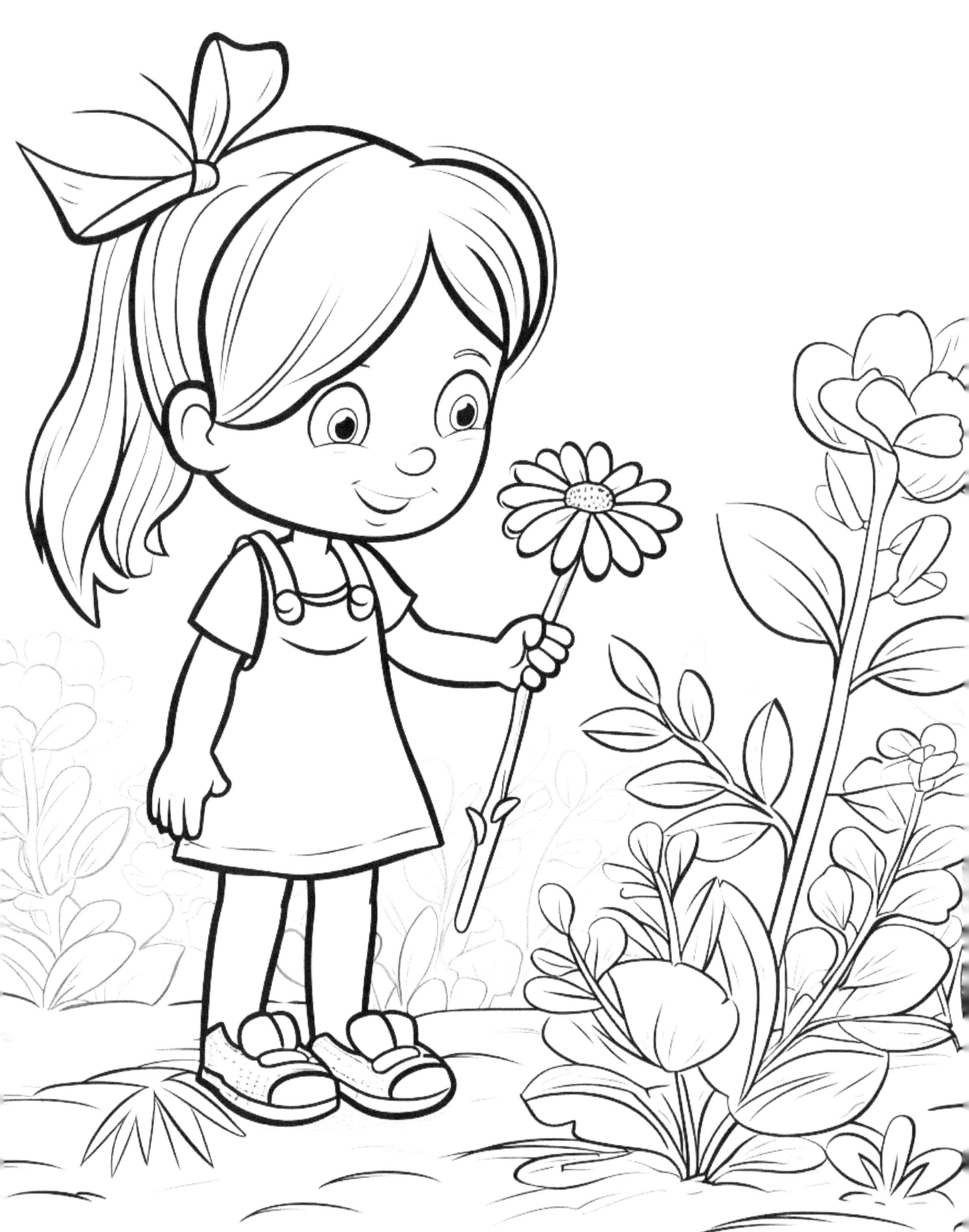

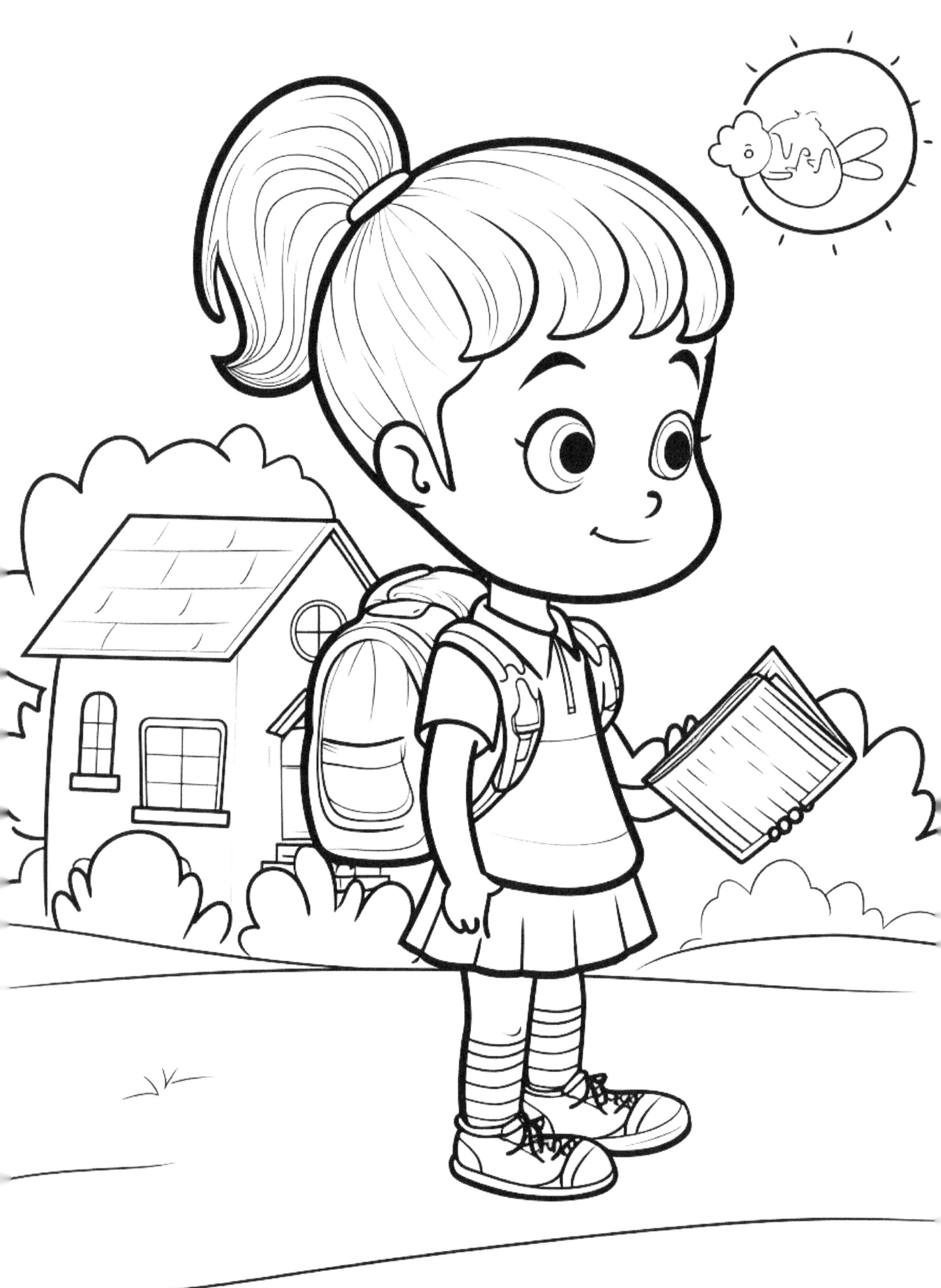

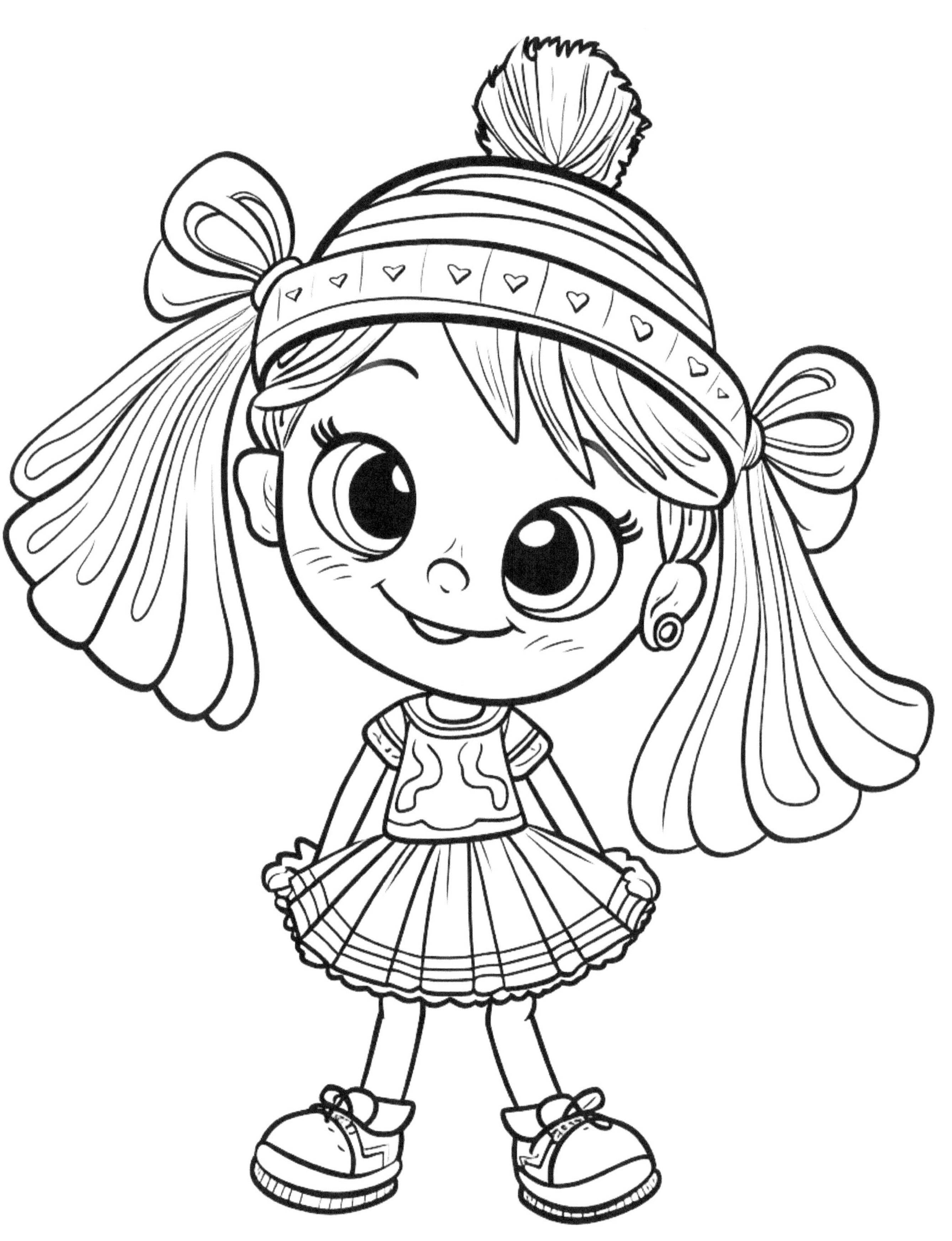

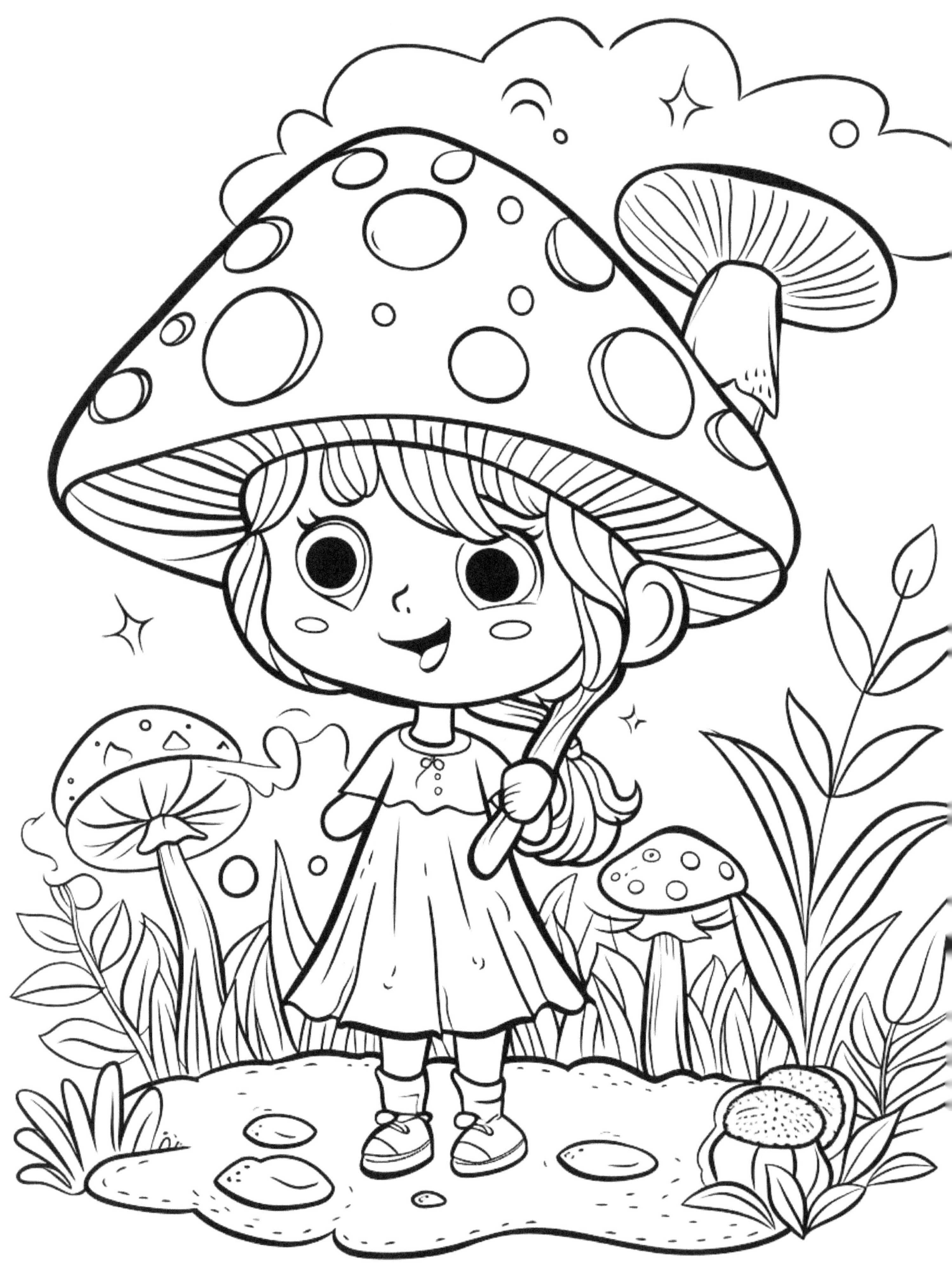

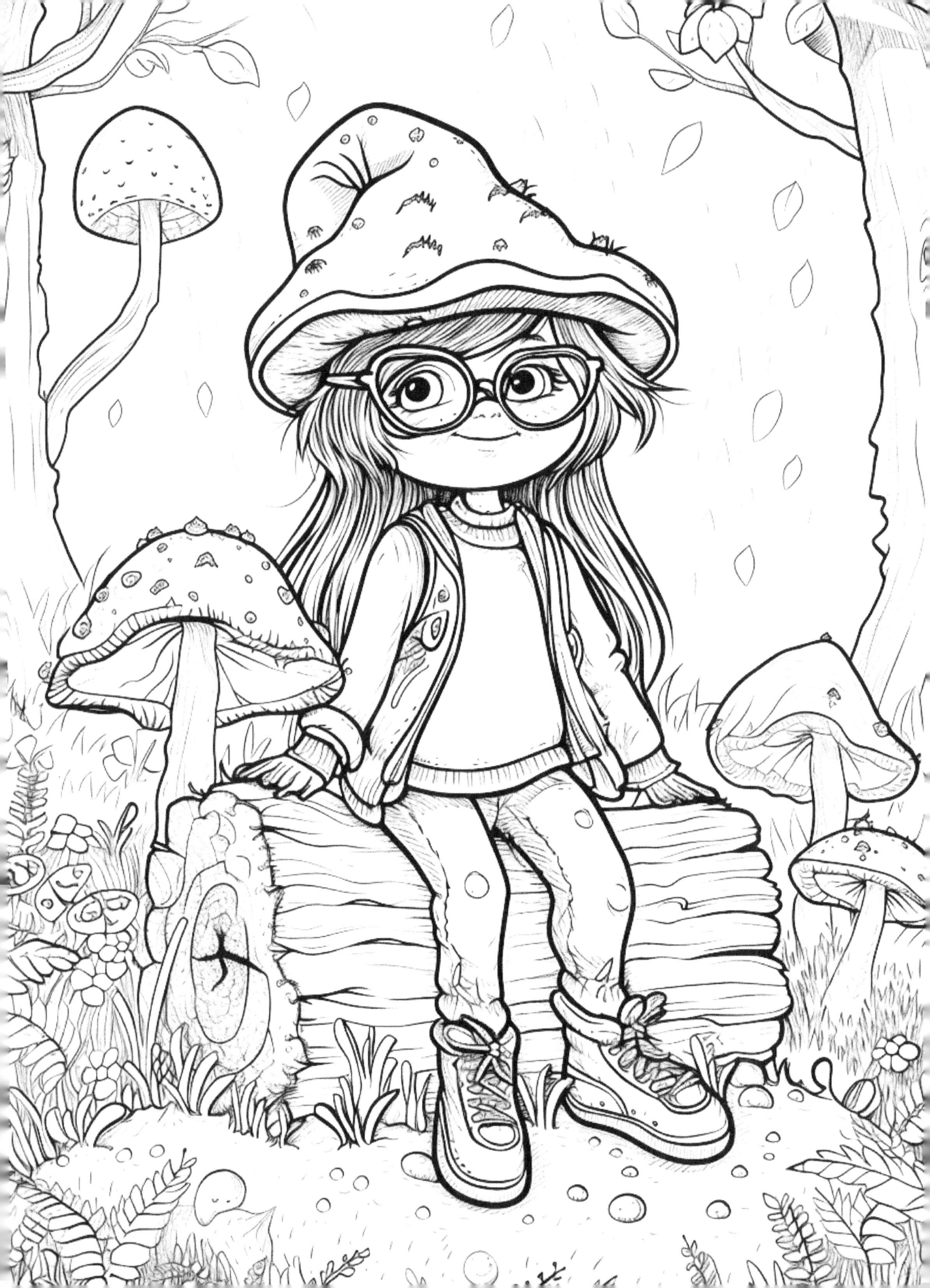

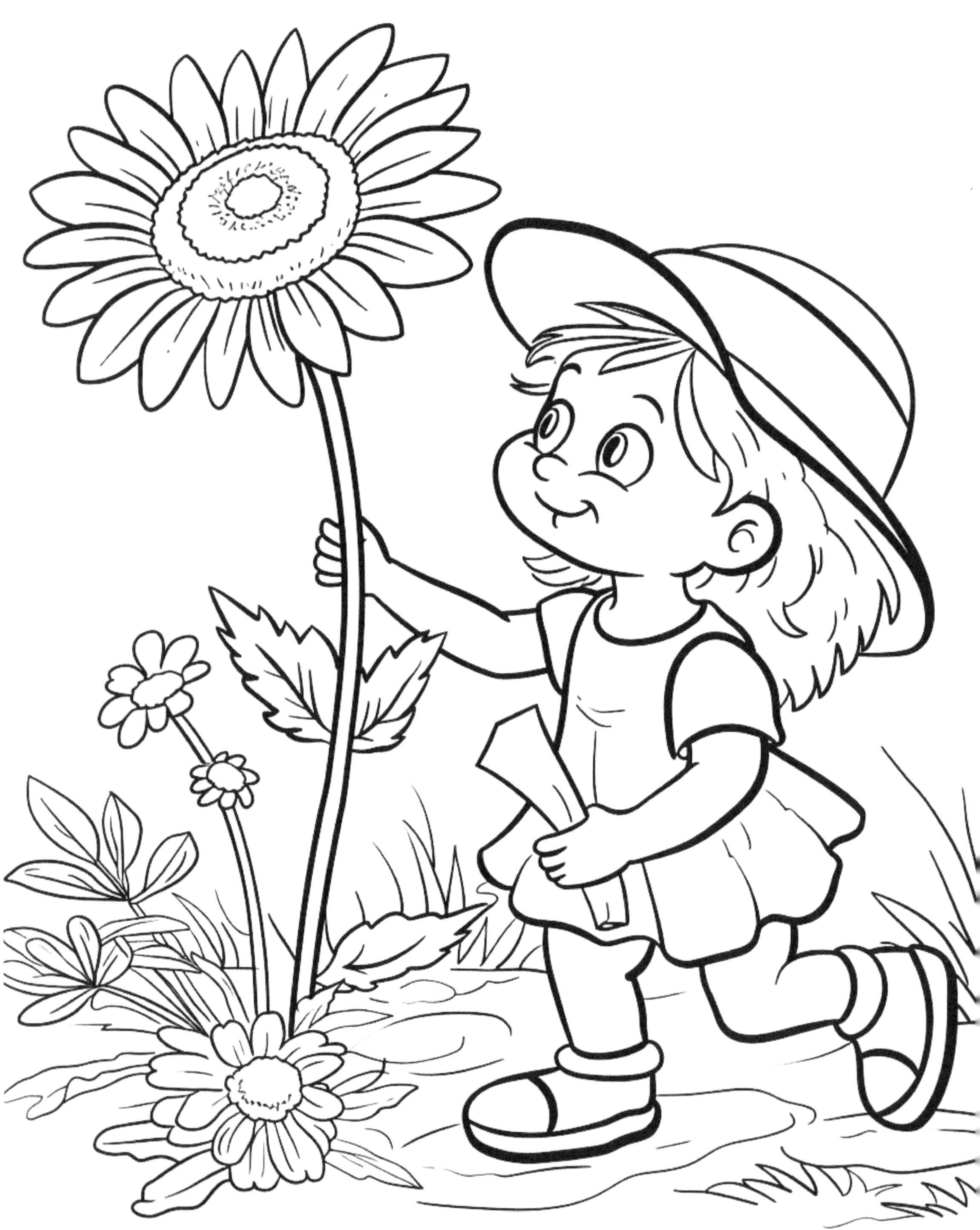

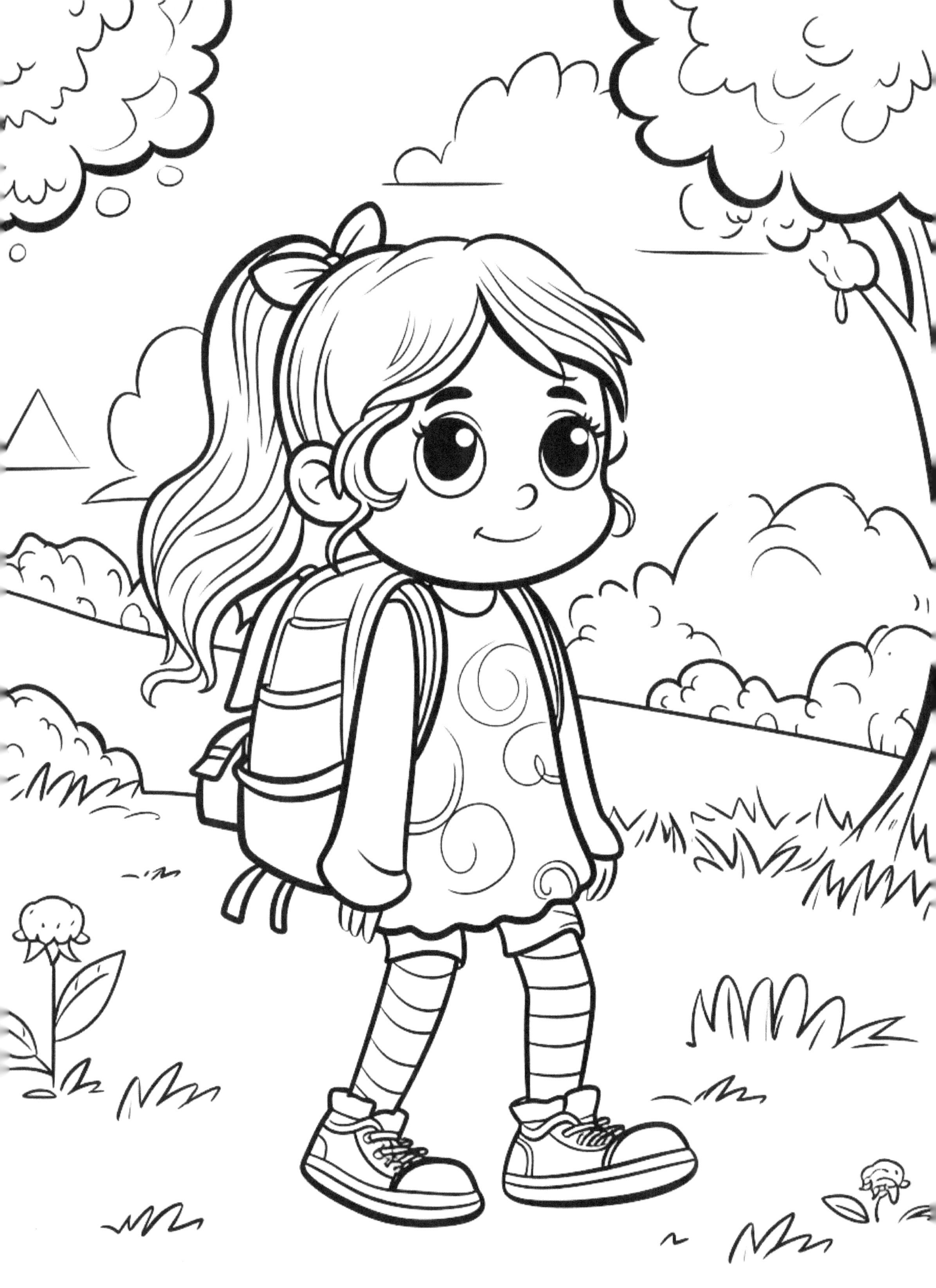

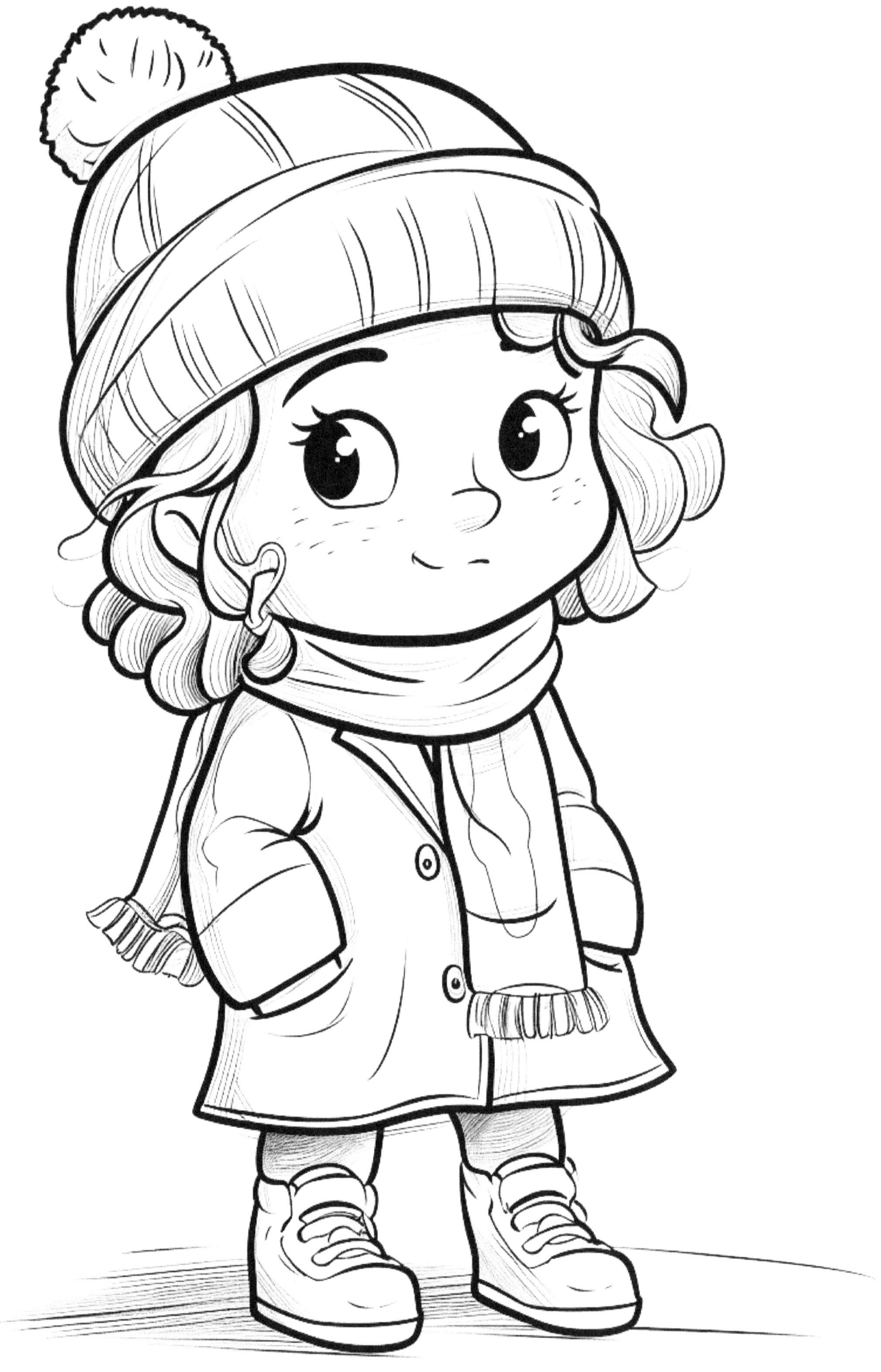

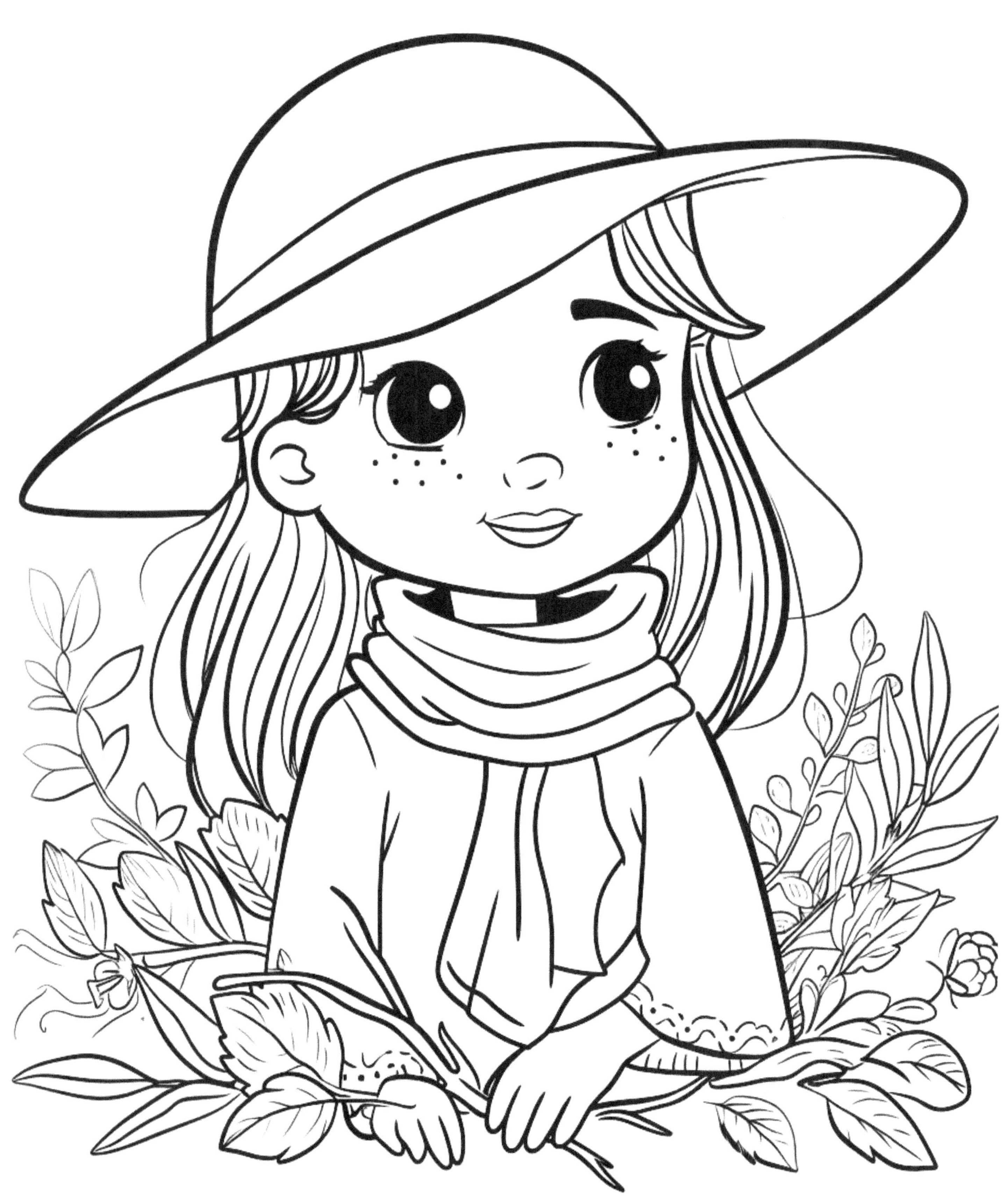

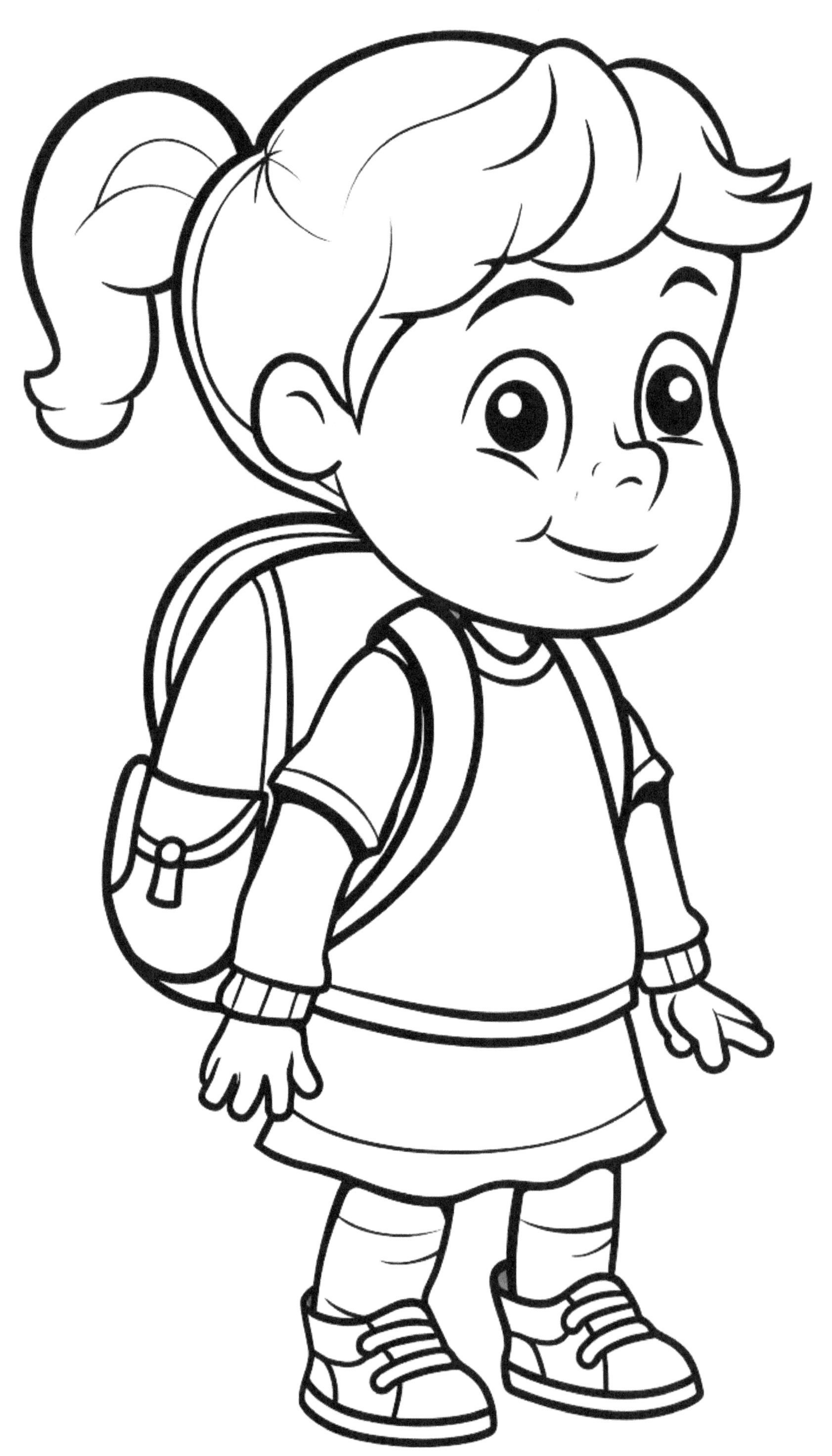

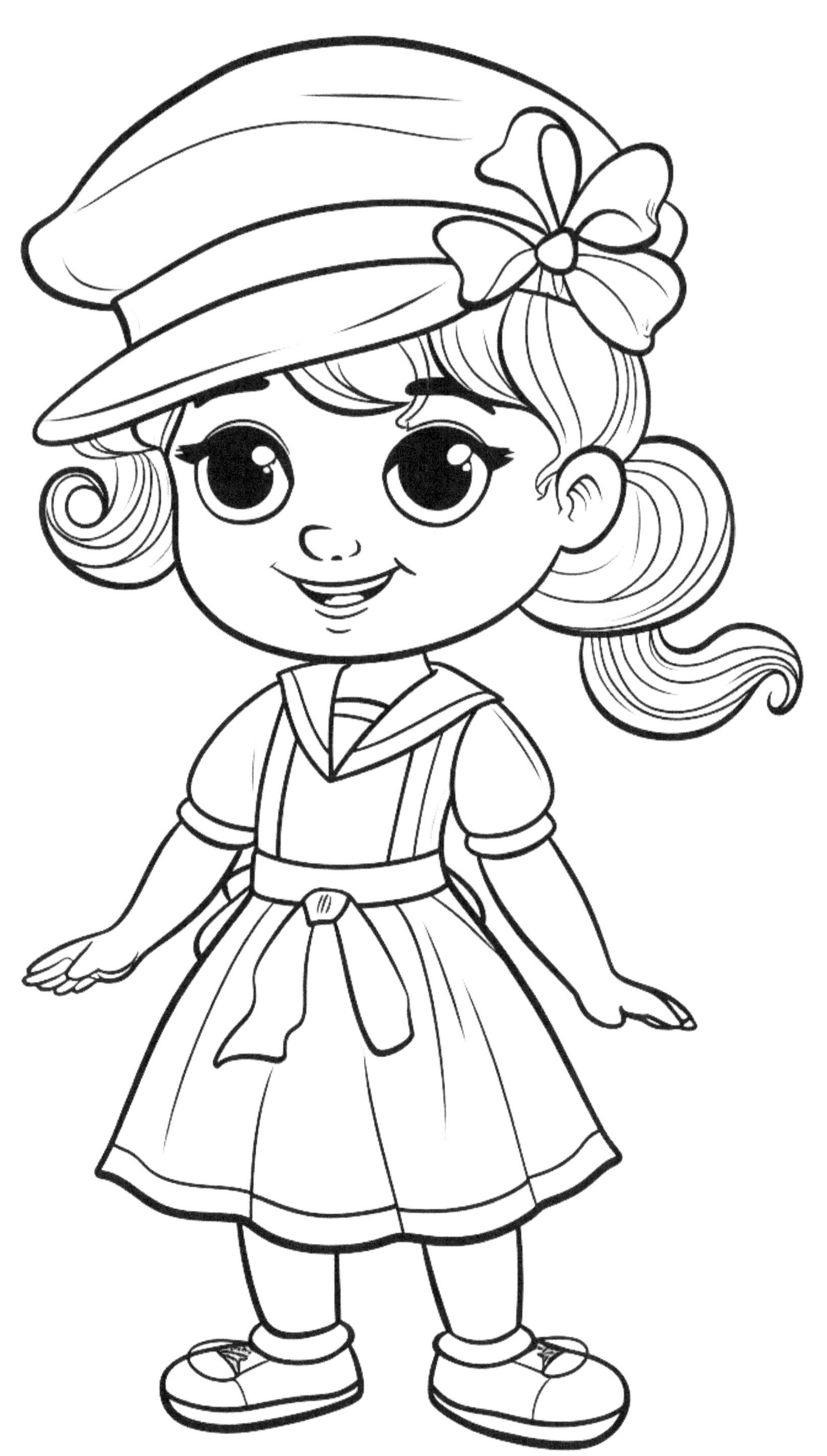

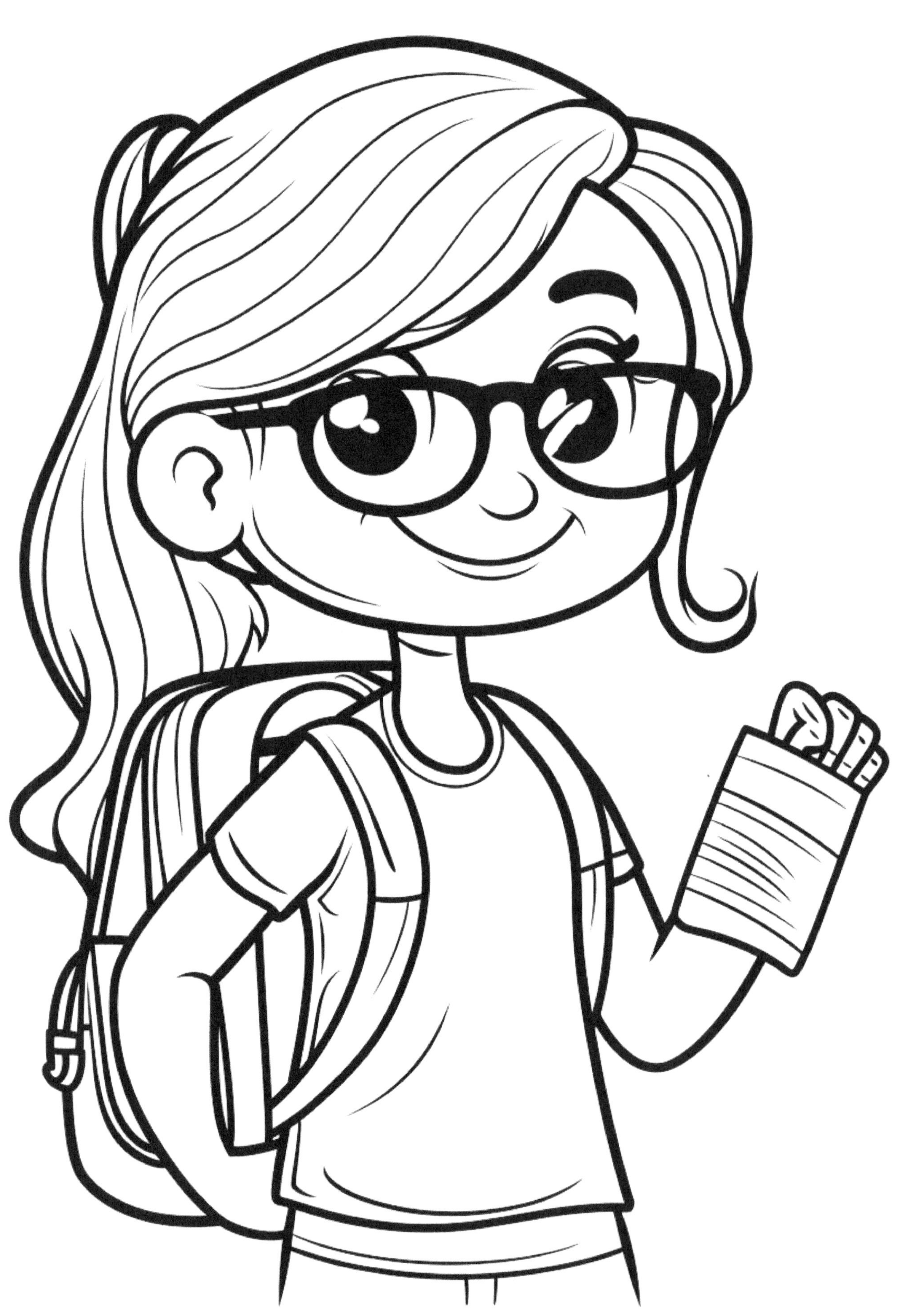

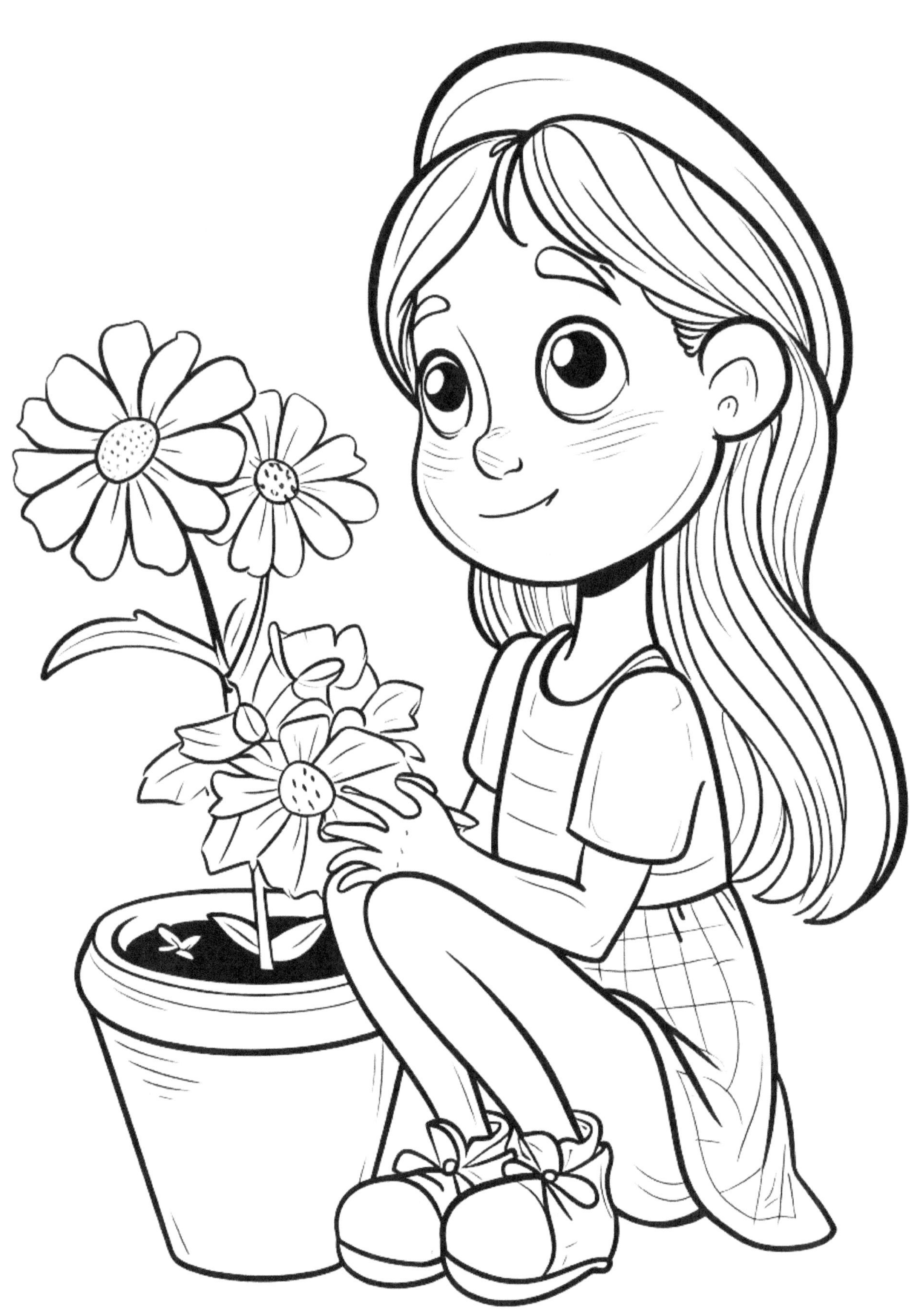

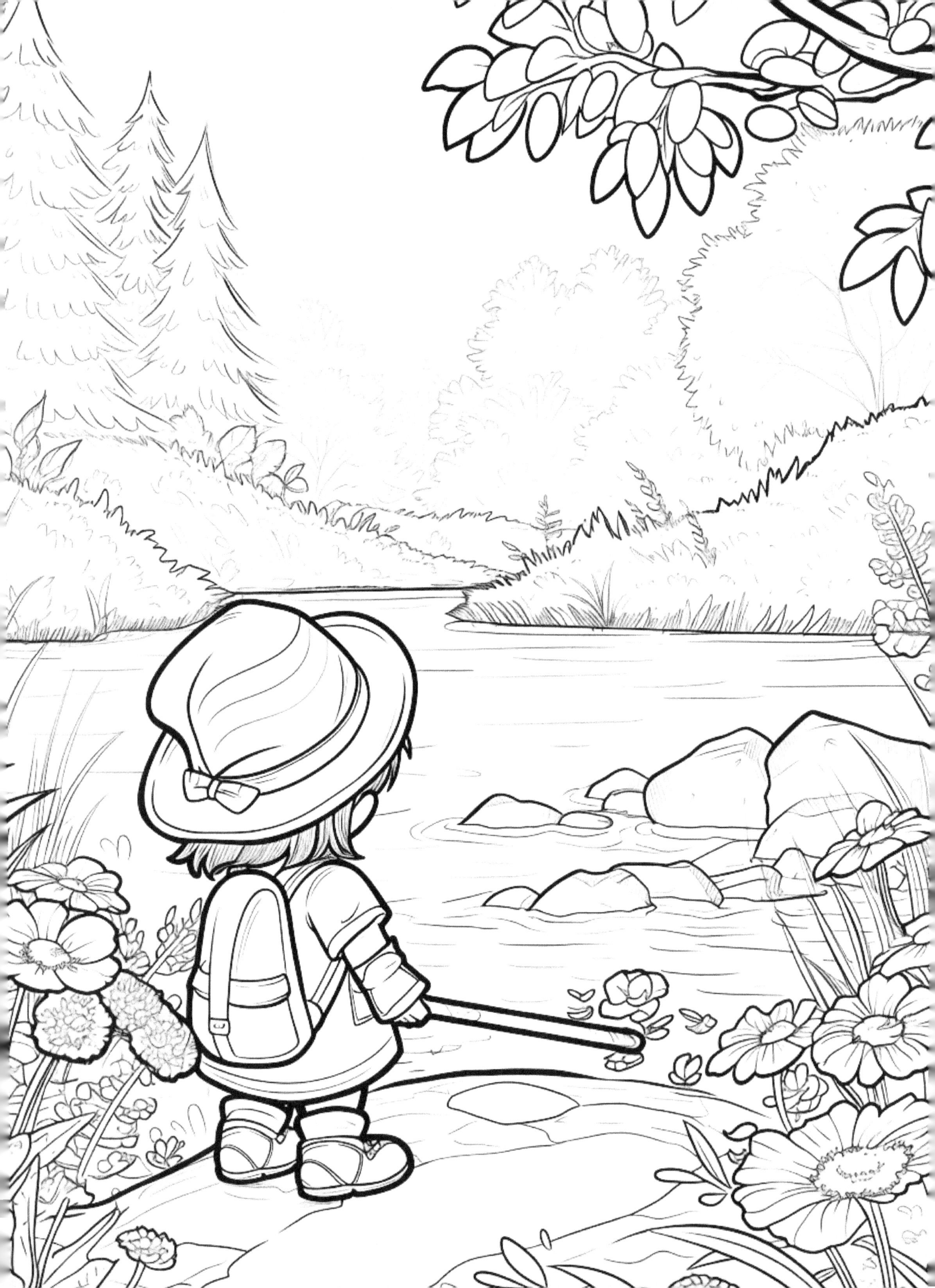

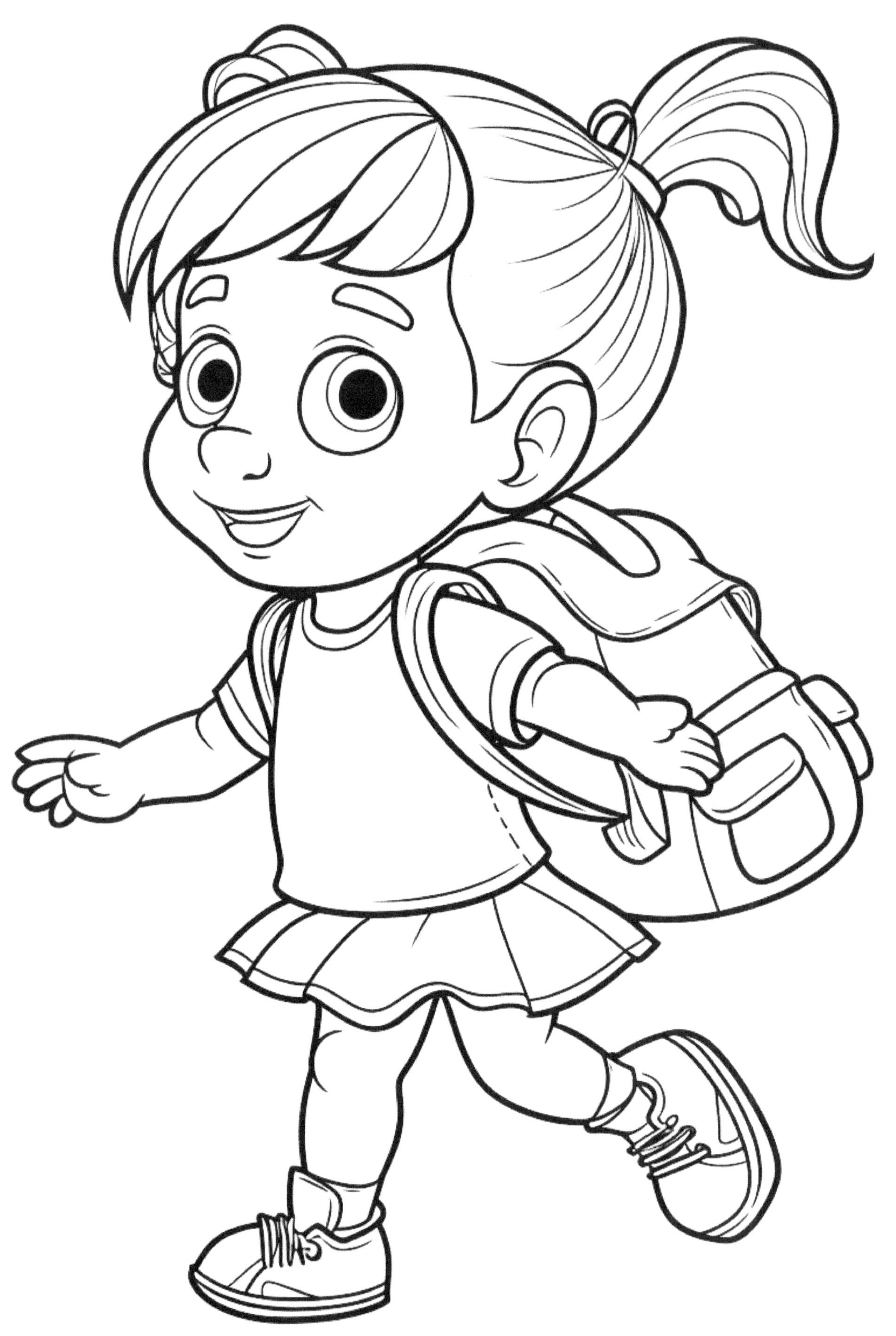

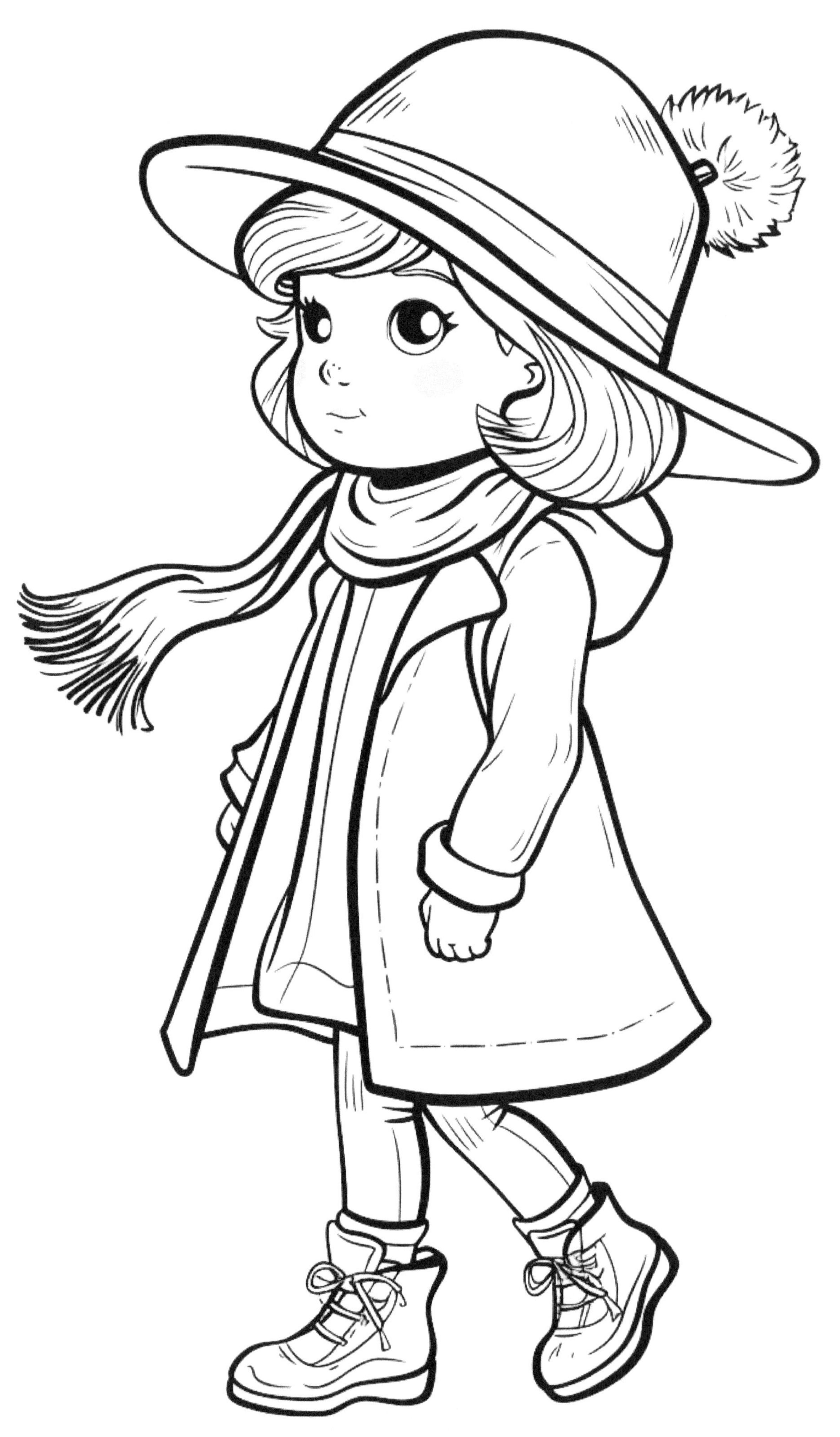

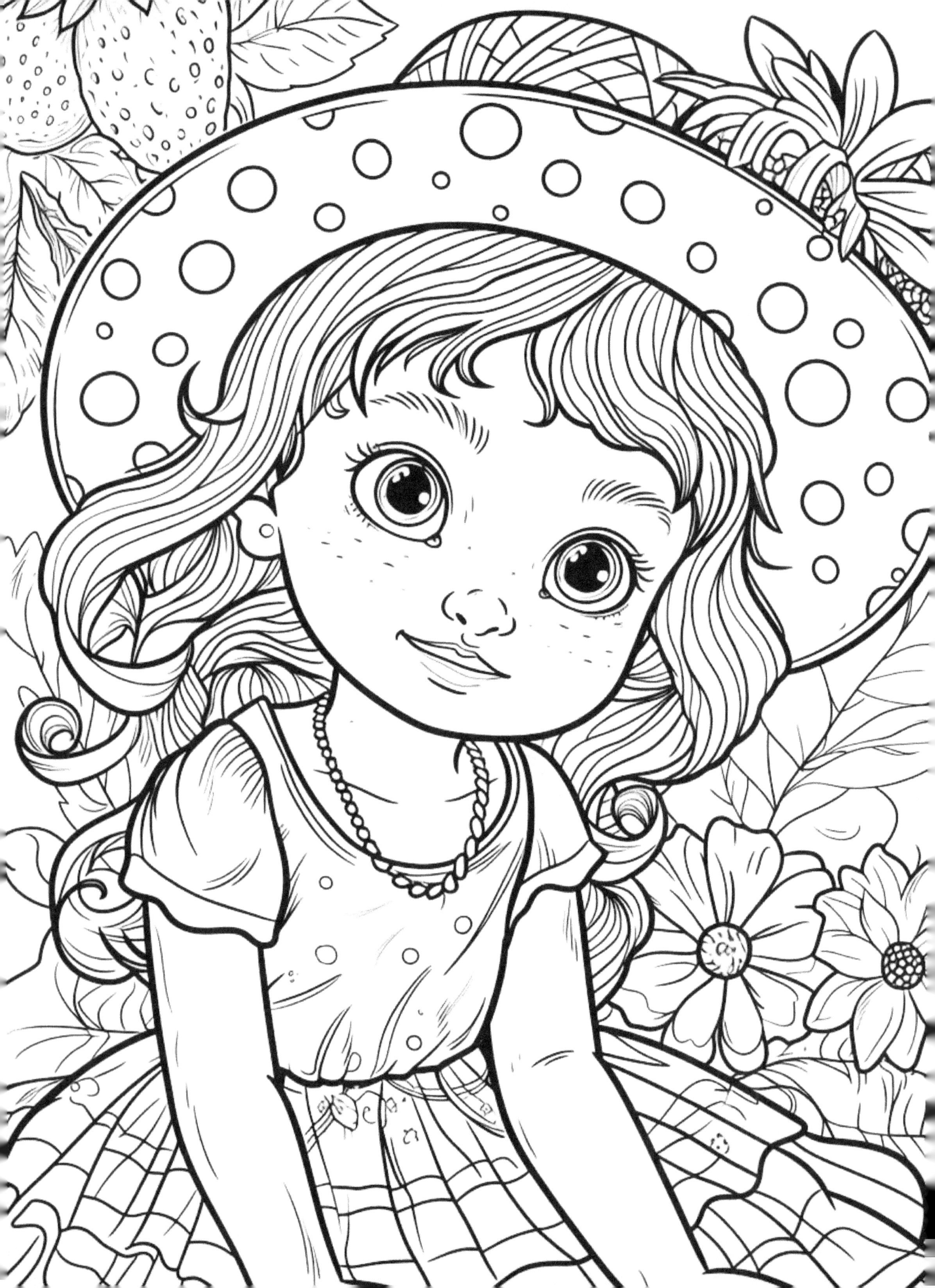

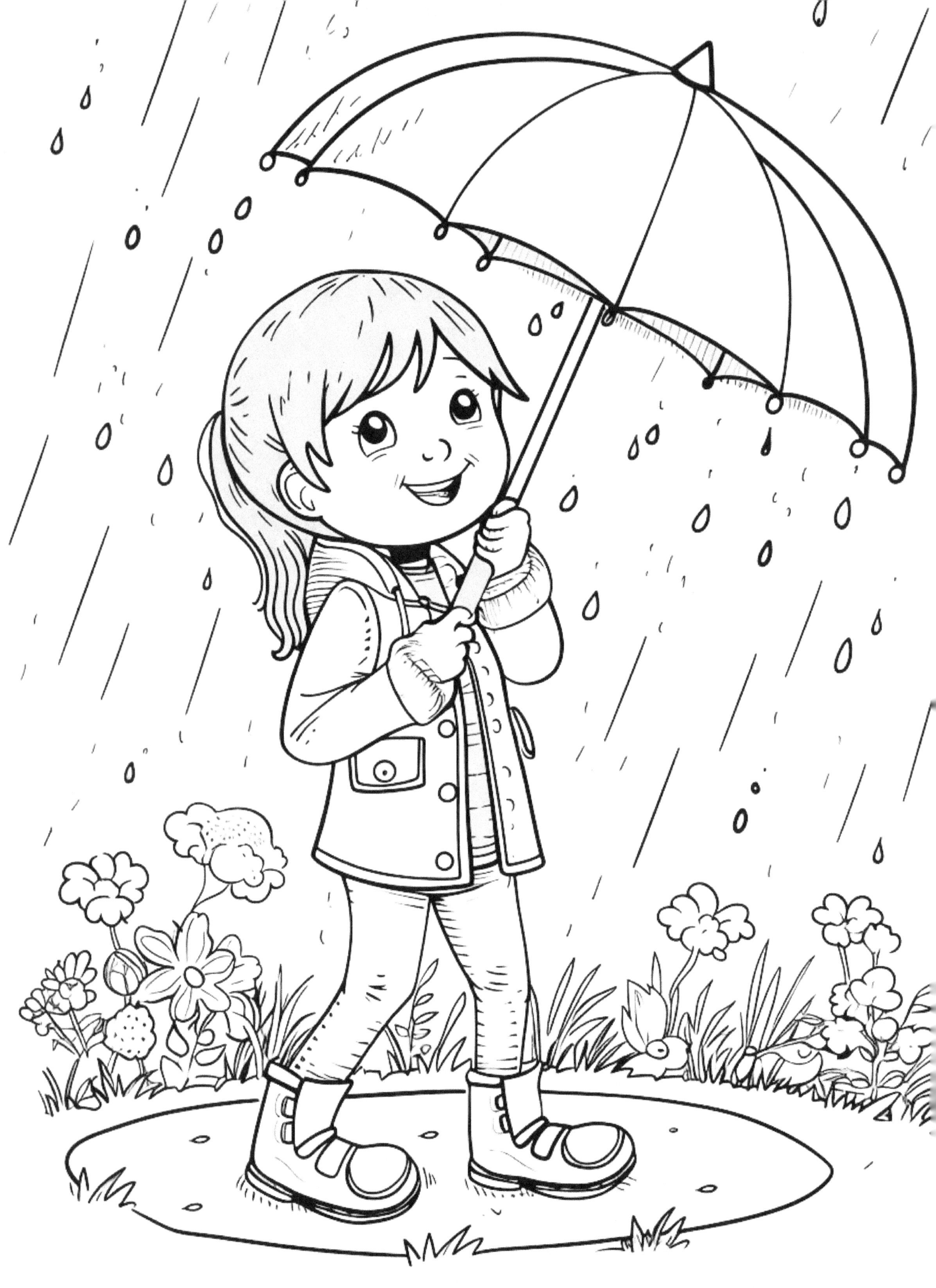

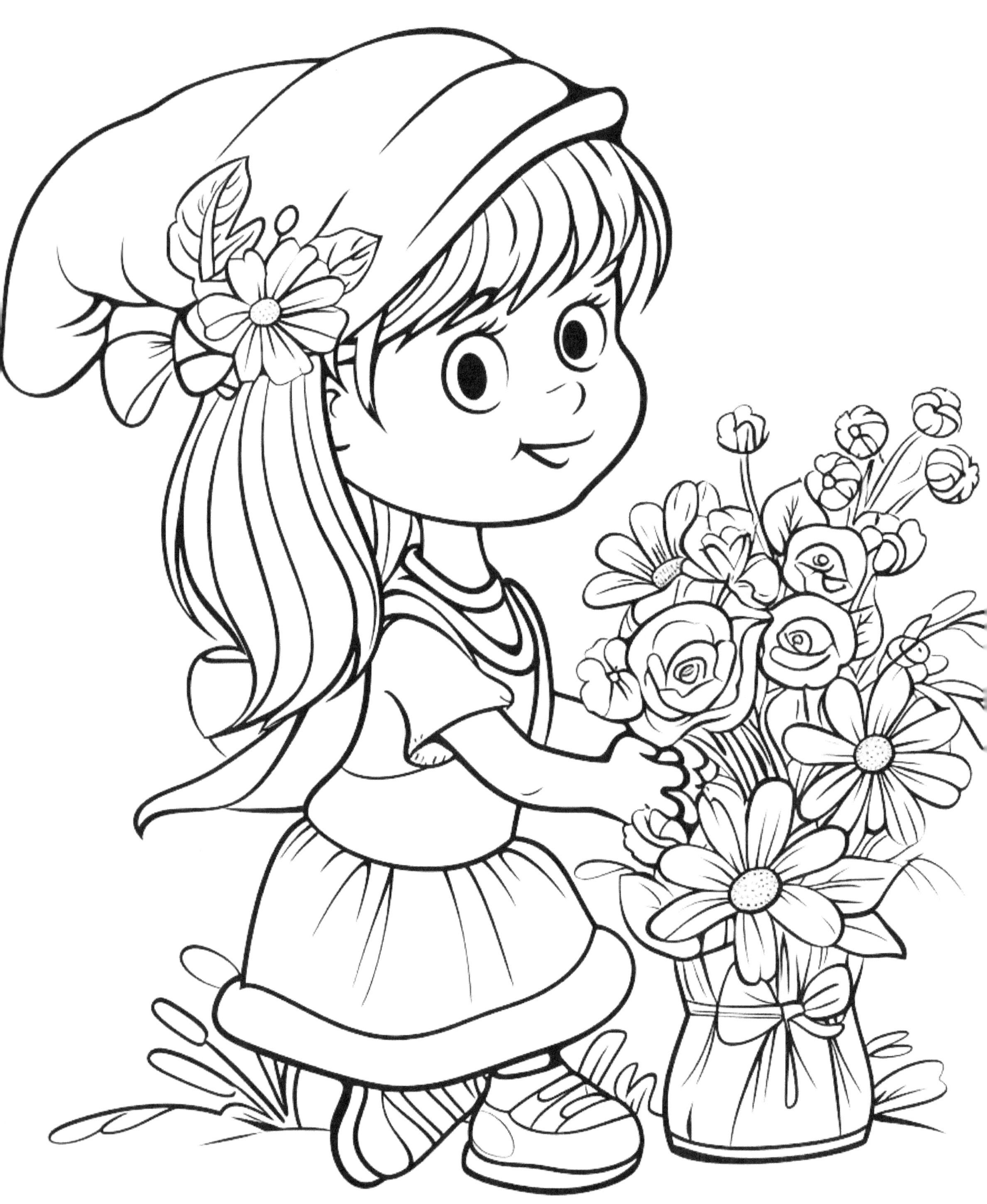

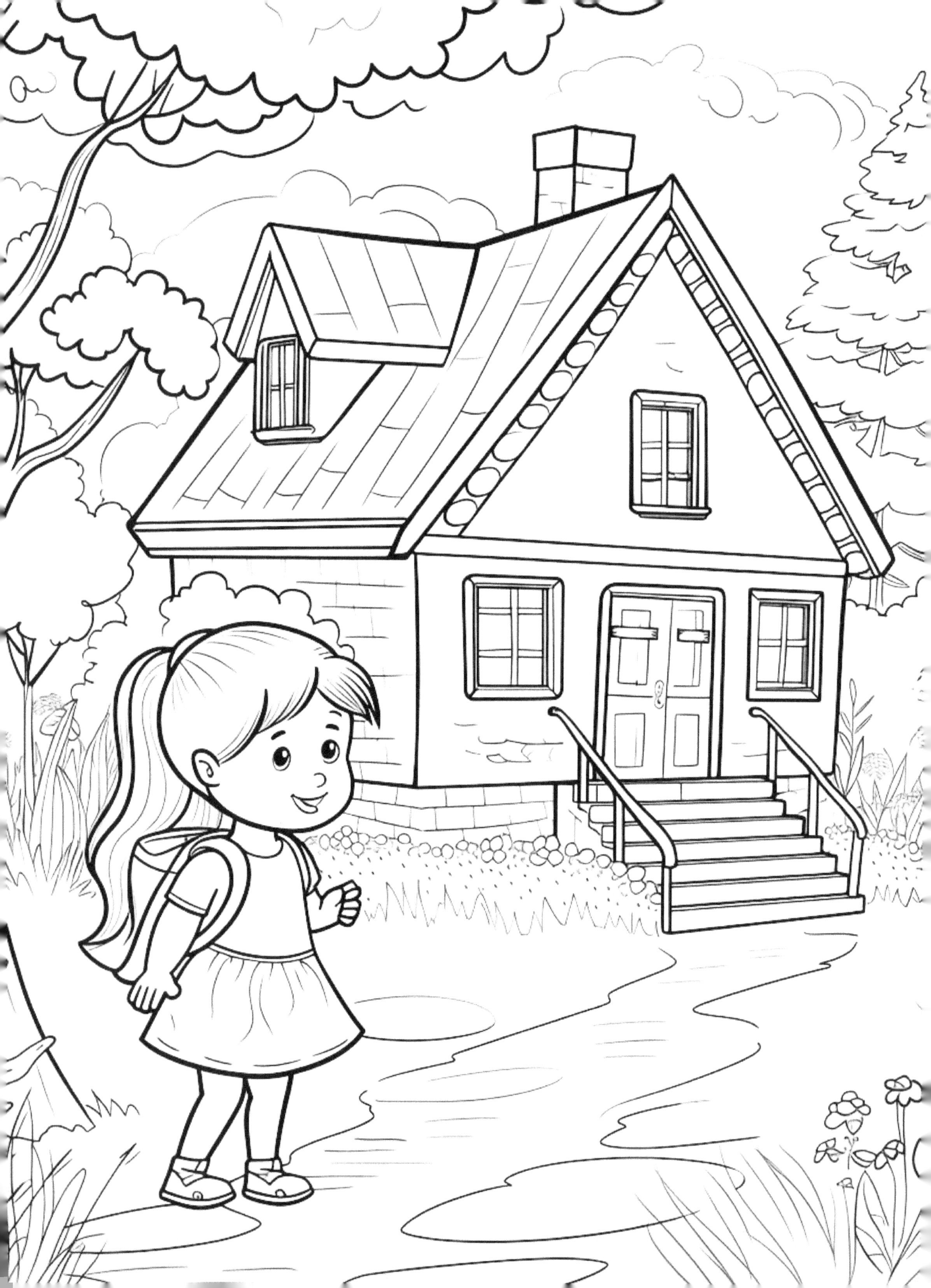

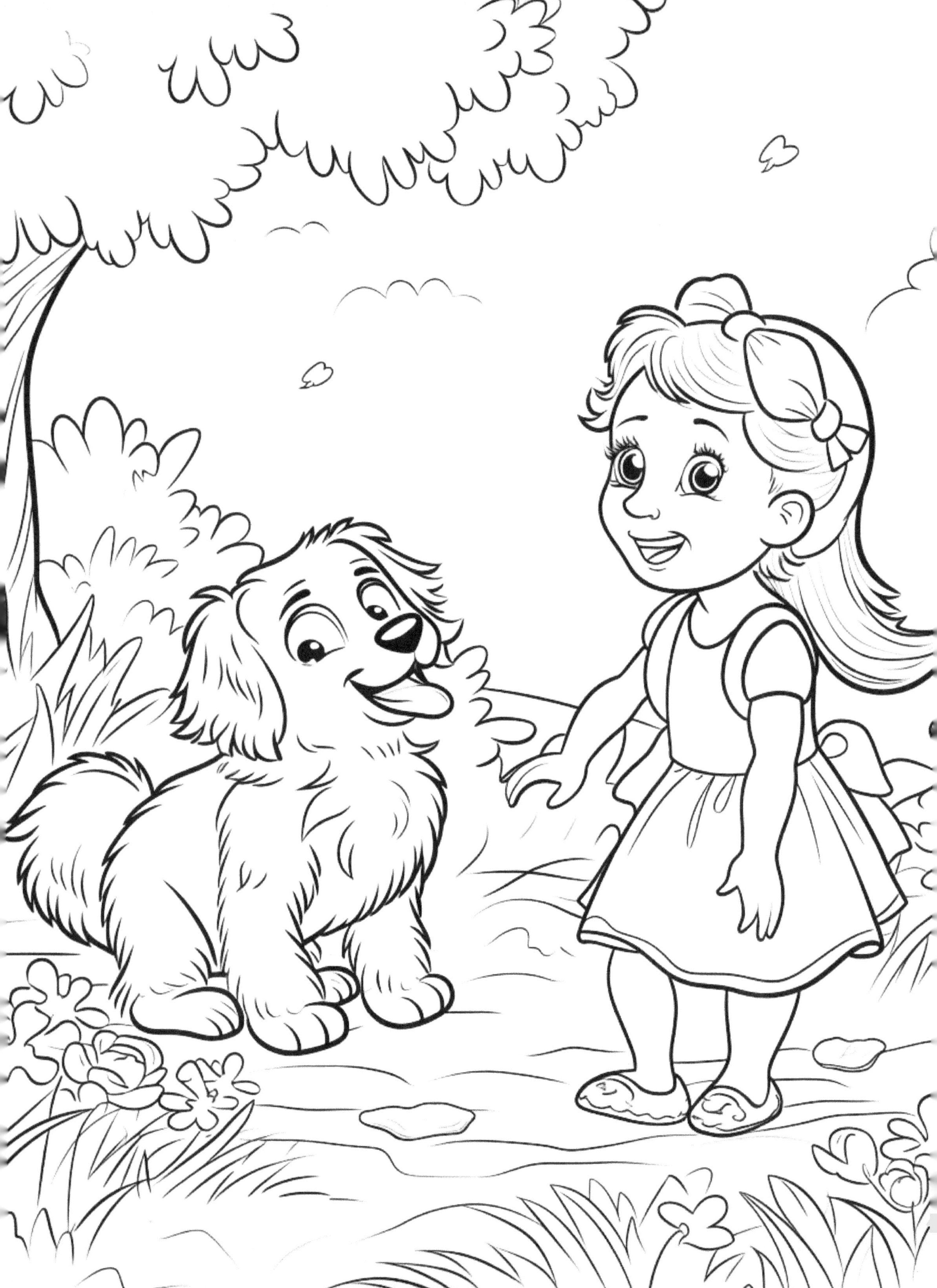

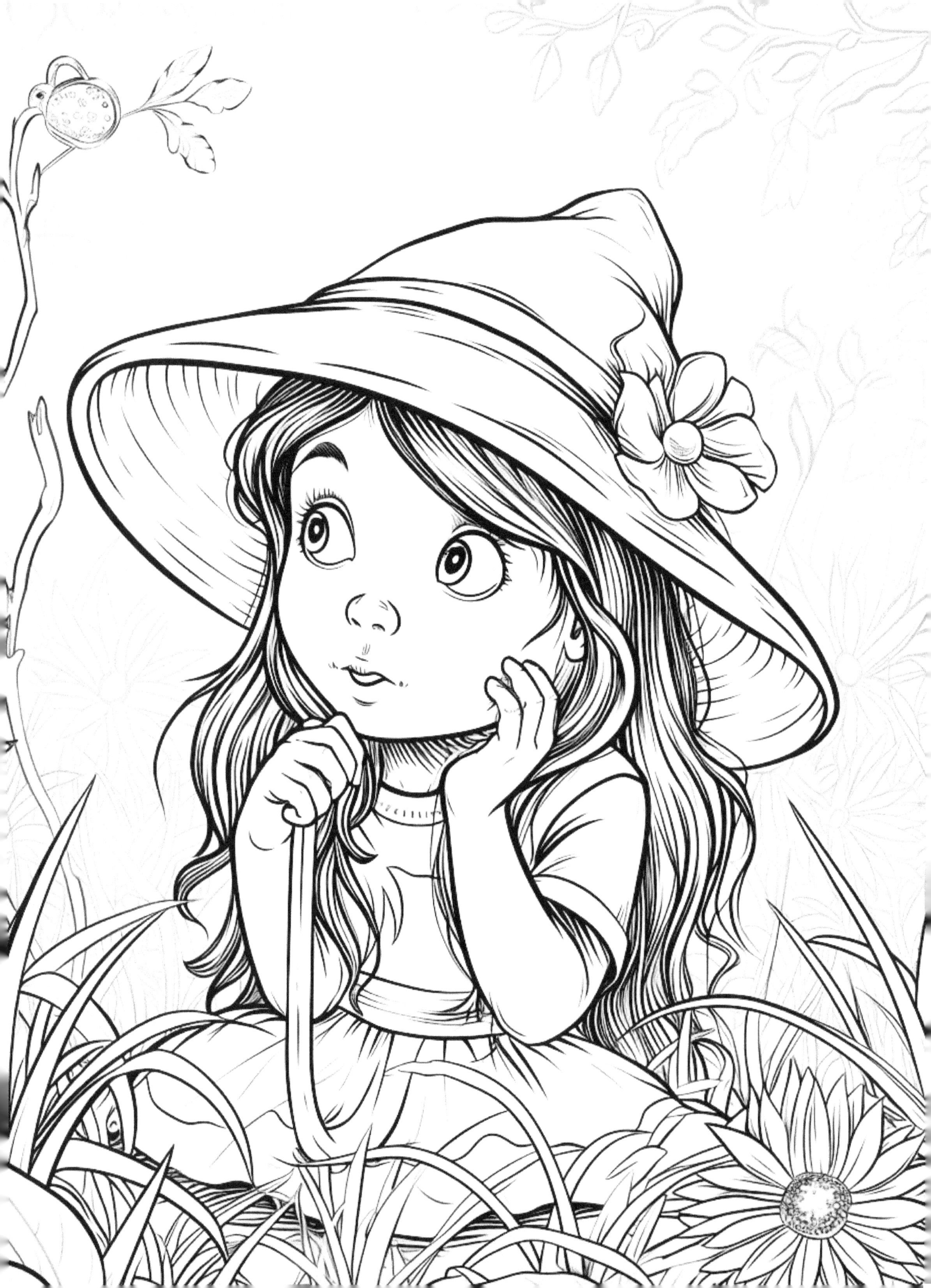

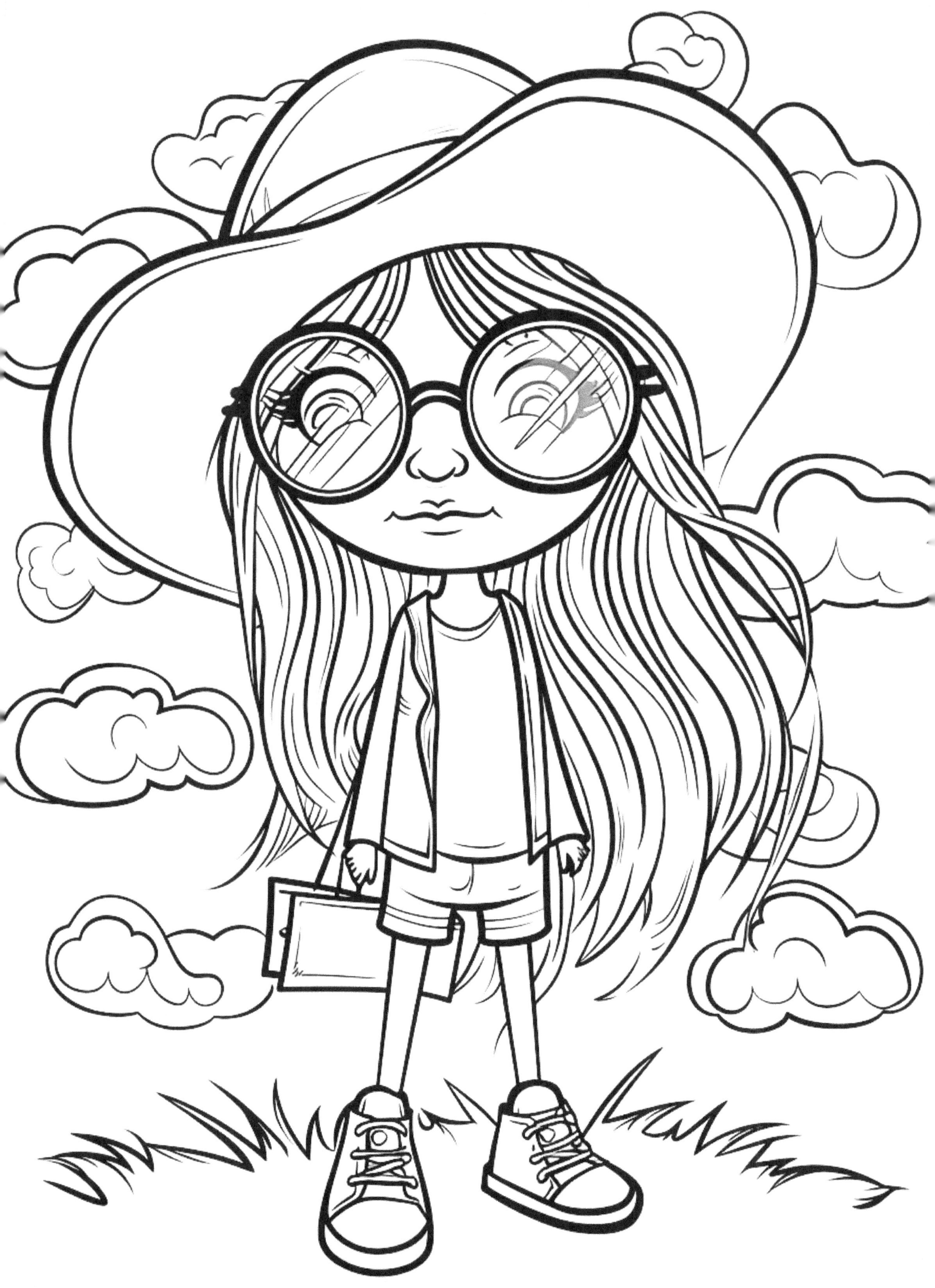

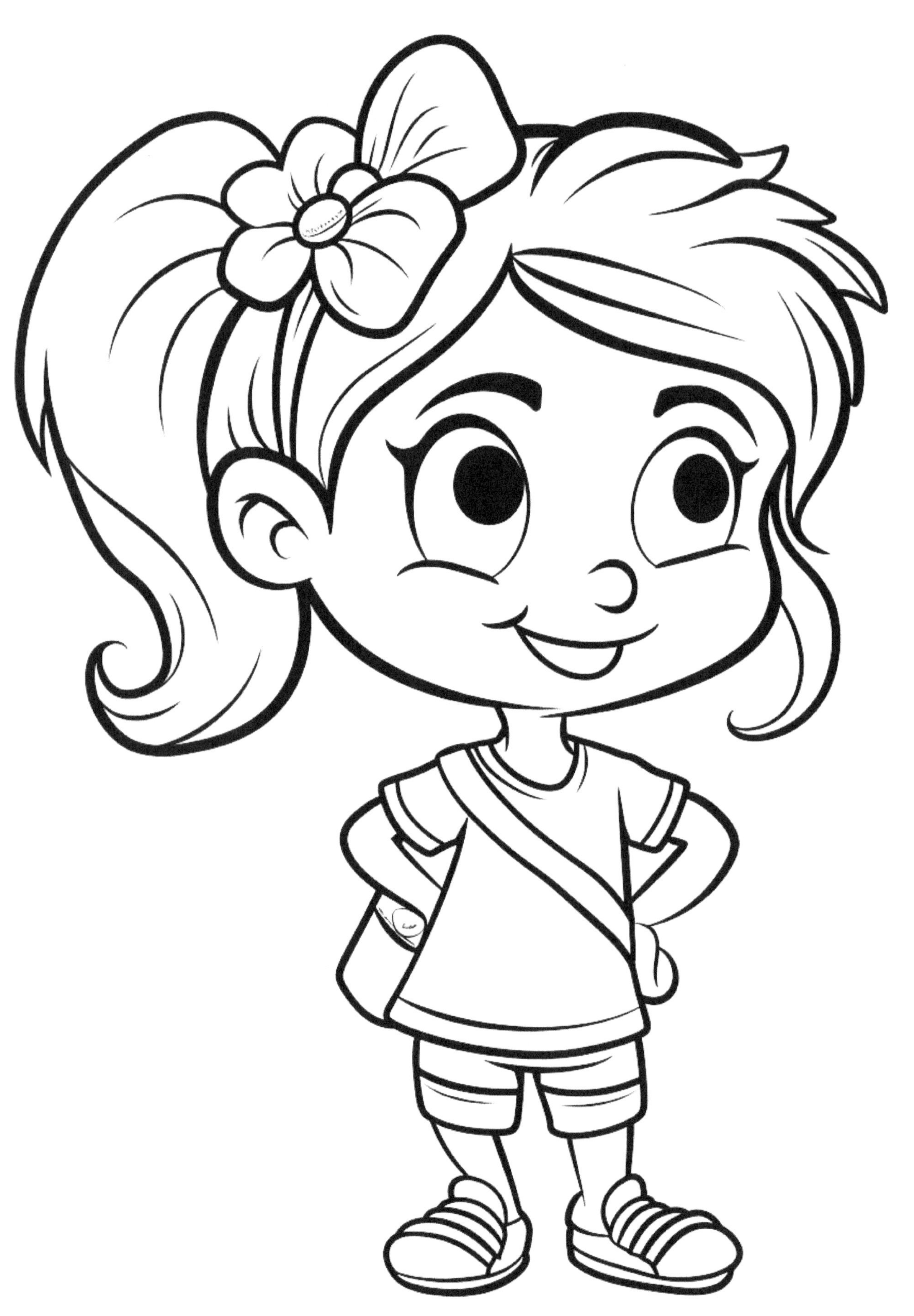

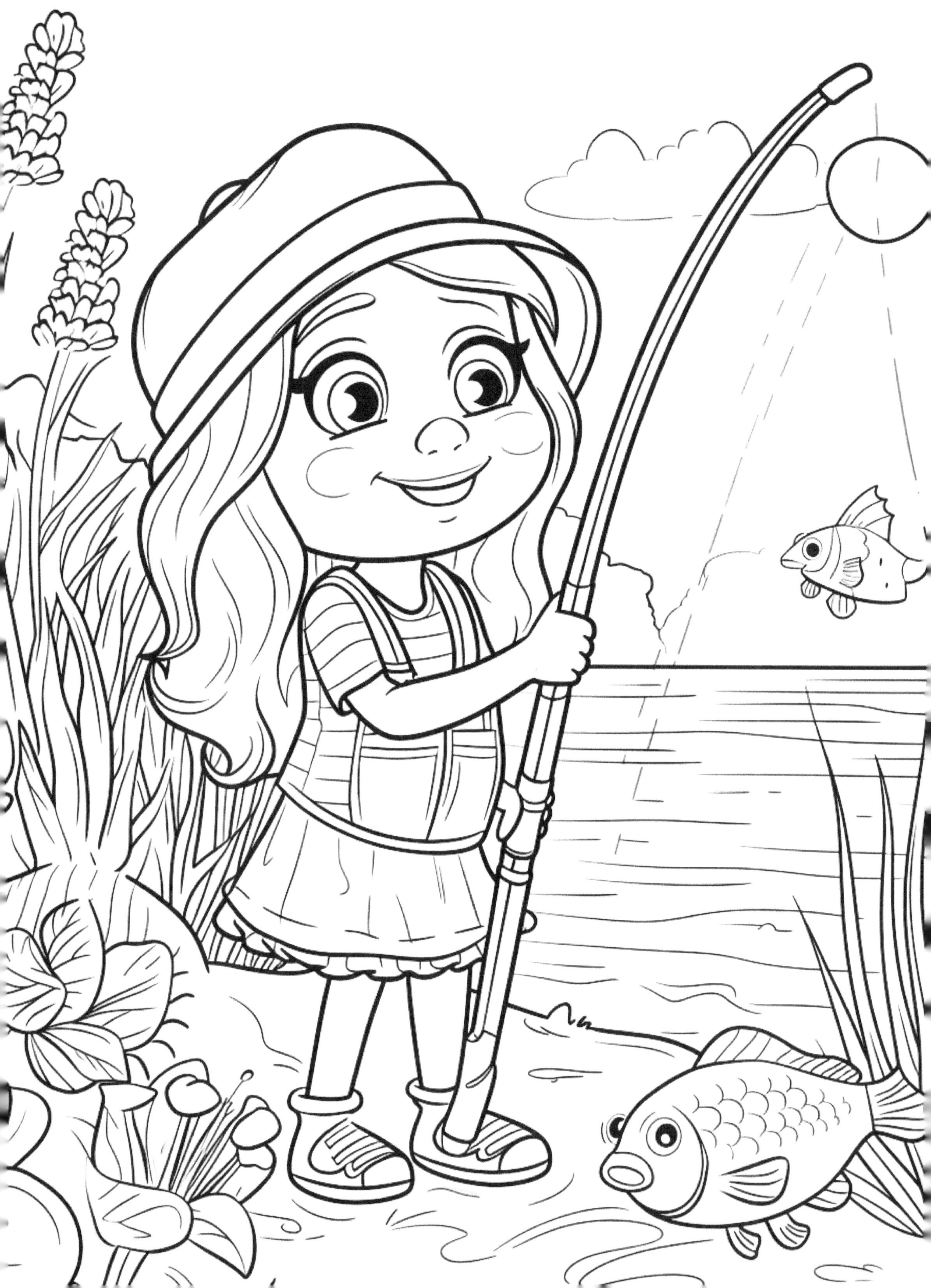

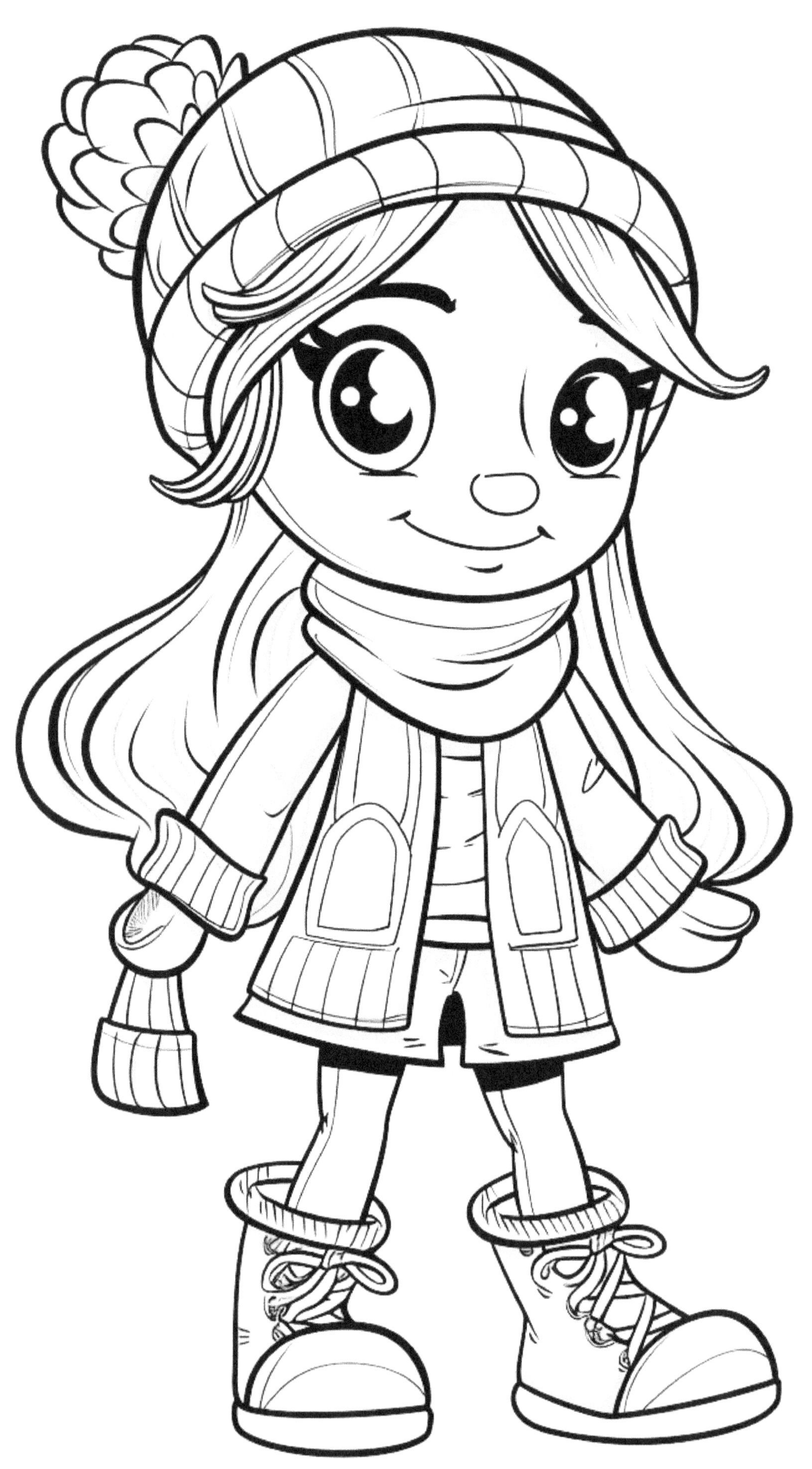

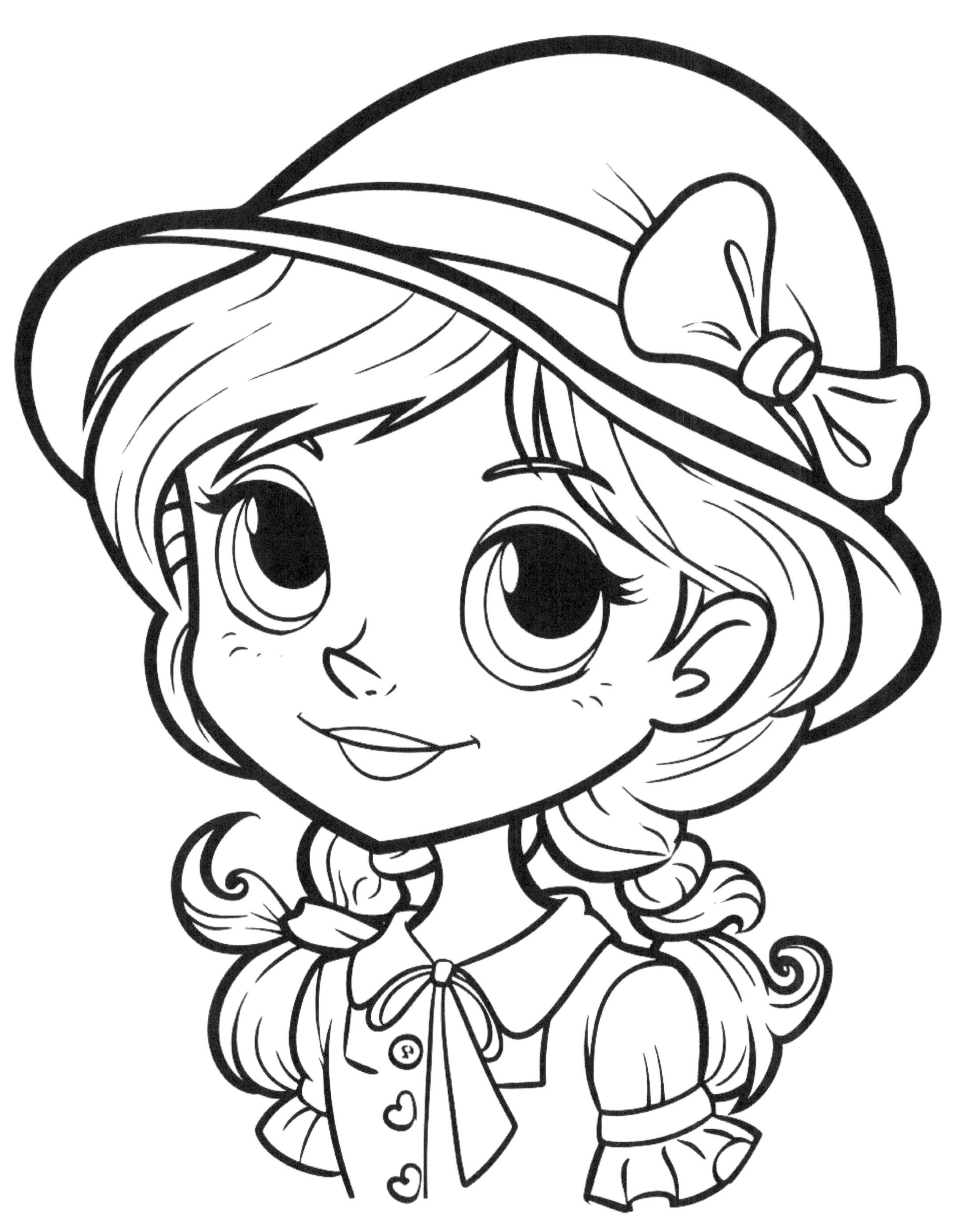

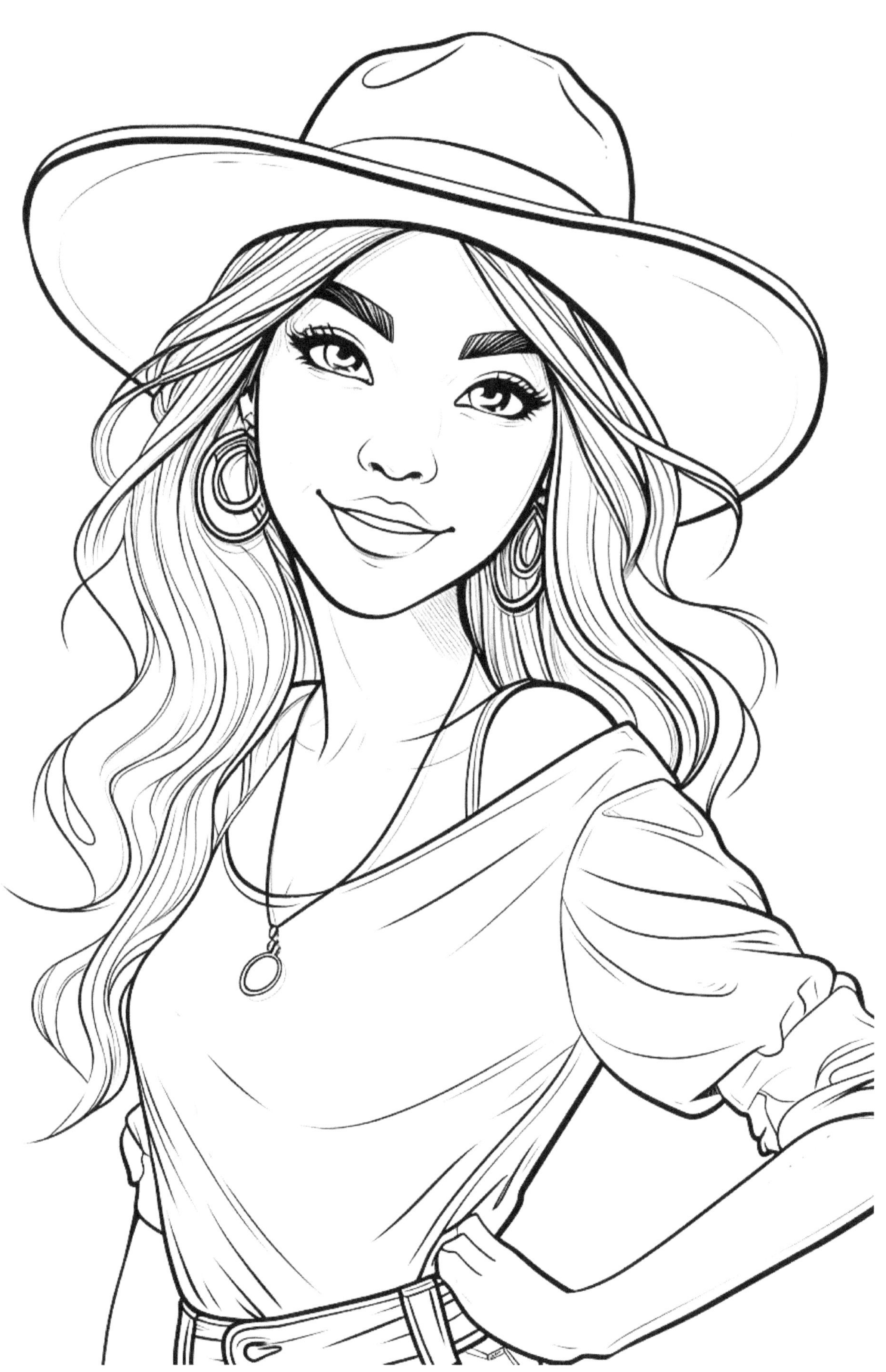

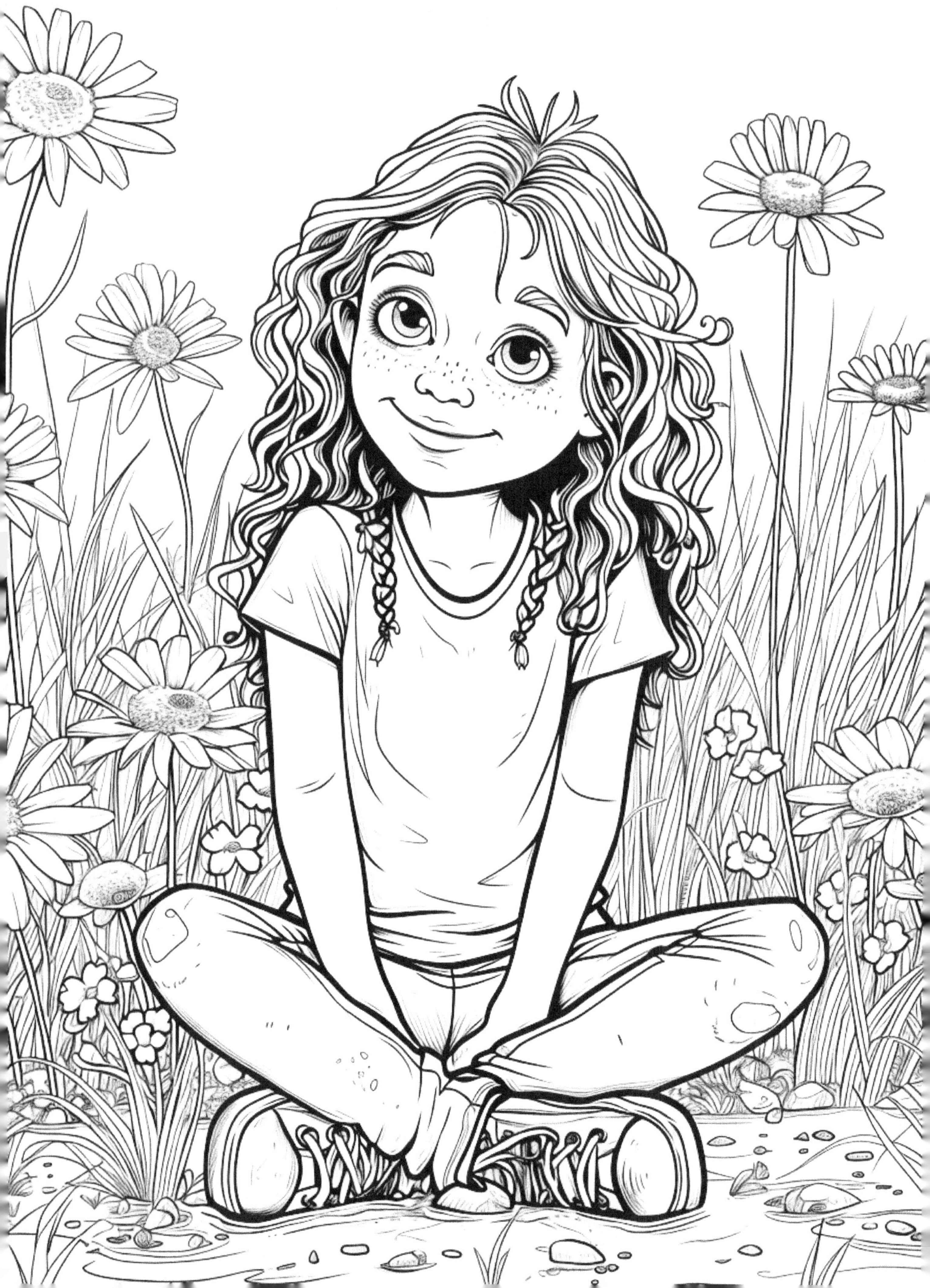

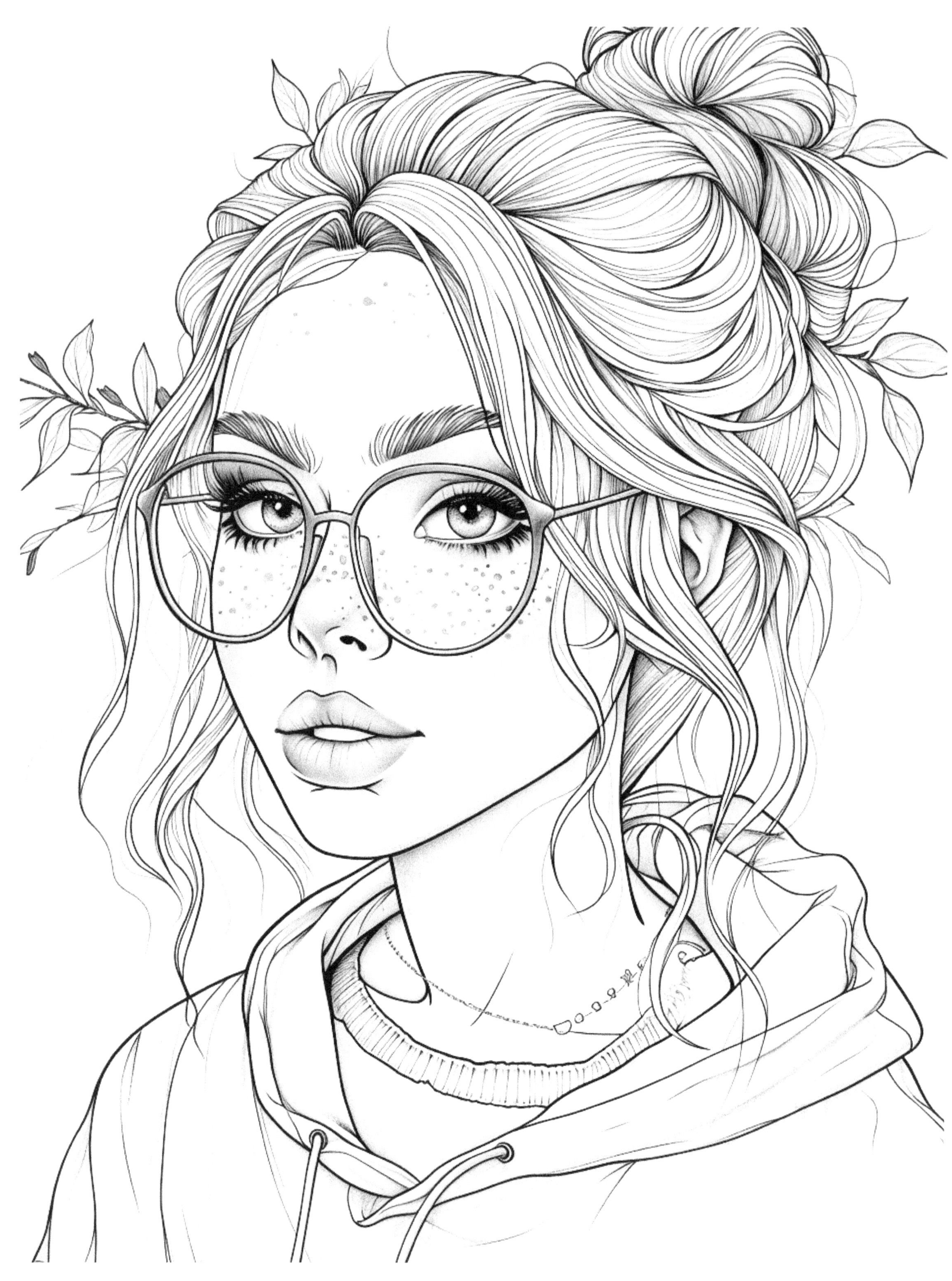

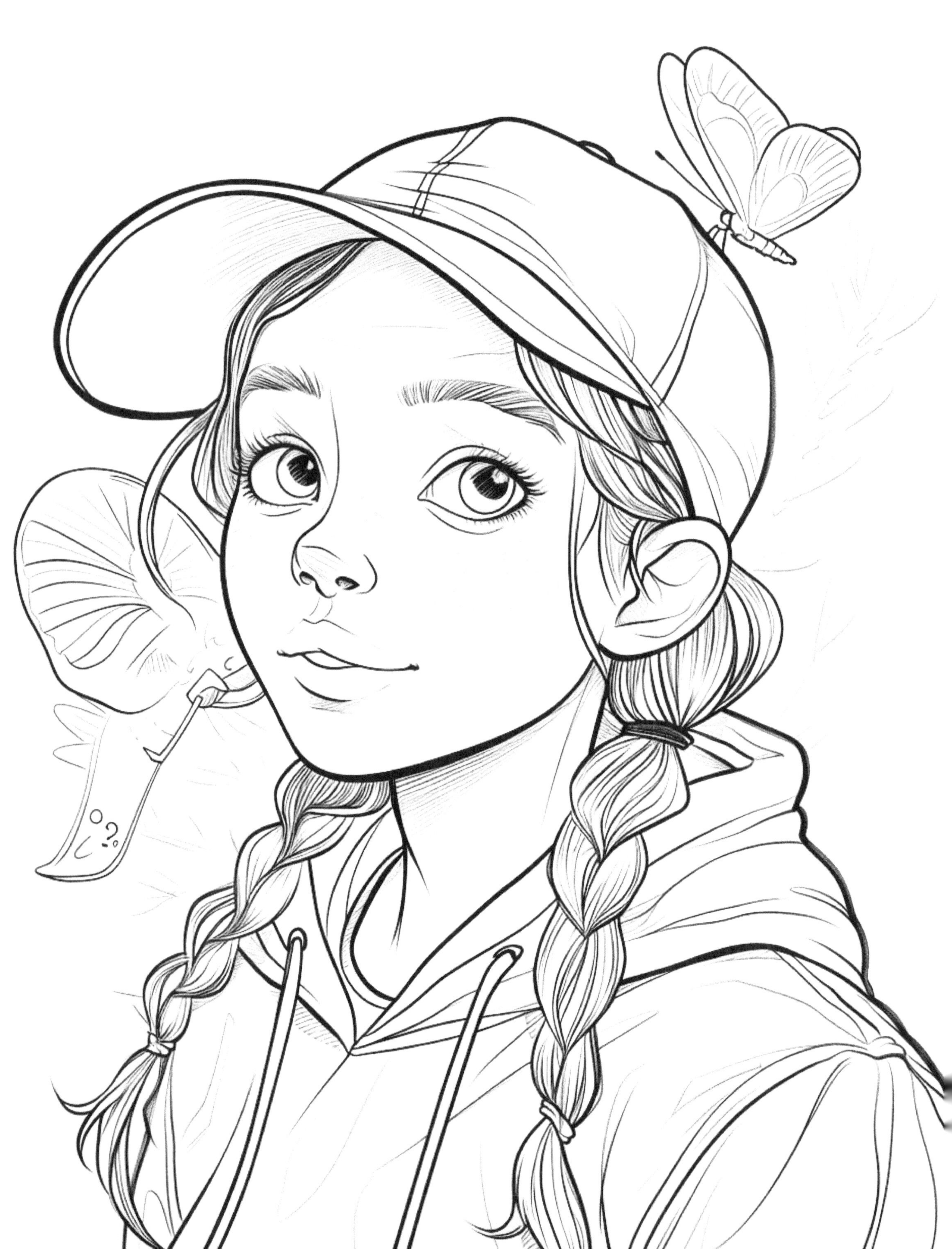

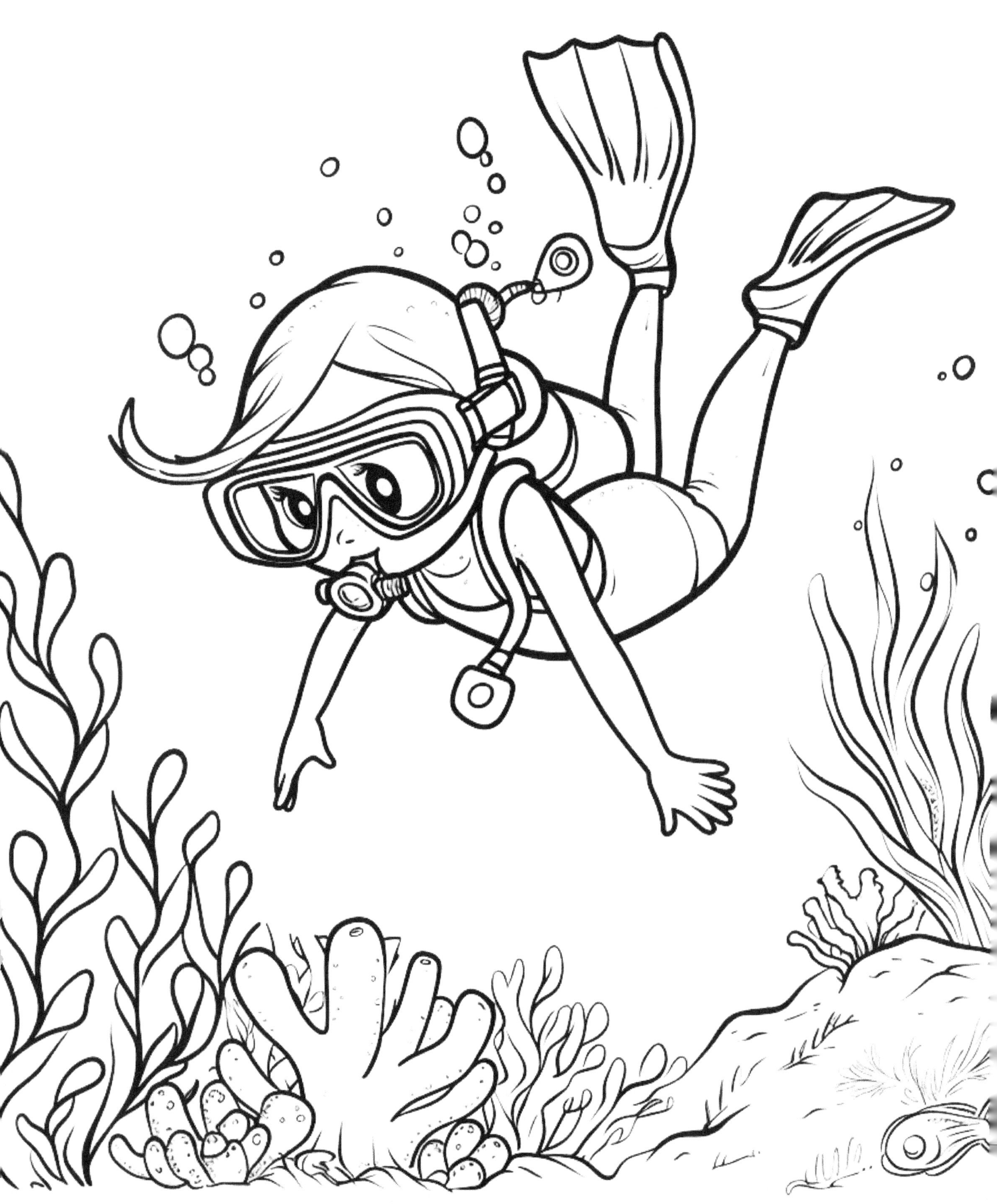

You've conquered mountains, explored oceans, and dreamed big with these amazing girls!

I hope you enjoyed bringing them to life with your unique colors and imagination.

Remember, you have the power to embark on your own incredible adventures, no matter how big or small.

Keep dreaming, keep exploring, and keep sharing your creativity! Share your colorful creations with us leave a review with your picture on Amazon. I'd love to see your masterpieces!

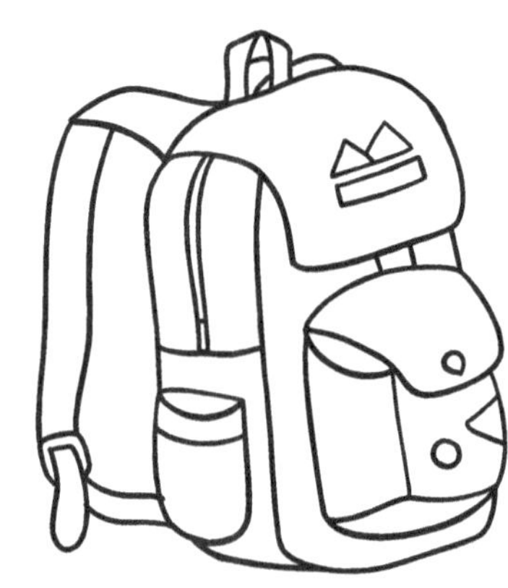

With warm wishes,
Artur Sobolevskij